MW00617966

Praise for *Jungle Warfare*

"Athletes, salespeople, and Christians—we are called to persevere regardless of what is thrown our way. As a Dallas Cowboy, I learned to tackle that lesson first hand. Chris' book reminds us of the best of what all champions know—there's no quit in a winner. Read this and you'll remember you really can 'do all things through Christ who gives you strength.'"

— **Bill Bates**
NFL All-Pro and Pro-Bowl Player
Safety, Dallas Cowboys NFL Champions
(Superbowls XXVII, XXVIII, XXX)

"As Christians in this present world we find ourselves in constant warfare. Paul admonished all of us to 'fight the good fight.' In his book, *Jungle Warfare*, Christopher Cunningham tells us how to not only fight but how to actually win. This book is recommended reading for all who hope to be successful in their own battles, but especially for those Christians who are in the arena of sales. You will find yourself referring again and again to sections of this book to help you fight the good fight."

— **Tim Lee**
Evangelist
Marine Sergeant from the jungles
 of Vietnam
www.timlee.org

JUNGLE WARFARE

A Basic Field Manual for Christians in Sales

Christopher A. Cunningham

"A 22-day Power-Packed Battle Plan"

THOMAS NELSON
Since 1798

NASHVILLE   DALLAS   MEXICO CITY   RIO DE JANEIRO

Published in Nashville, Tennessee, by Thomas Nelson. Thomas Nelson is a registered trademark of Thomas Nelson, Inc.

Thomas Nelson, Inc., titles may be purchased in bulk for educational, business, fund-raising, or sales promotional use. For information, please e-mail SpecialMarkets@ThomasNelson.com.

Unless otherwise noted, Scripture quotations are taken from the HOLY BIBLE: NEW INTERNATIONAL VERSION® © 1973, 1978, 1984 by International Bible Society. Used by permission of Zondervan Publishing House. All rights reserved.

Scripture quotations marked NKJV are from THE NEW KING JAMES VERSION. © 1982 by Thomas Nelson, Inc. Used by permission. All rights reserved.

Scripture quotations marked ESV are from THE ENGLISH STANDARD VERSION. © 2001 by Crossway Bibles, a division of Good News Publishers.

Scripture quotations marked NLT are from the *Holy Bible*, New Living Translation, © 1996. Used by permission of Tyndale House Publishers, Inc., Wheaton, Illinois 60189. All rights reserved.

Scripture quotations marked MSG are from *The Message* by Eugene H. Peterson, © 1993, 1994, 1995, 1996, 2000. Used by permission of NavPress Publishing Group. All rights reserved.

Library of Congress Cataloging-in-Publication Data

Cunningham, Christopher A.
    Jungle warfare : a basic field manual for Christians in sales / Christopher A. Cunningham.
        p. cm.
    ISBN 978-1-59555-147-4
    1. Selling. I. Title.
HF5438.25.C86 2010
658.8'1—dc22   2009052636

Printed in the United States of America

10 11 12 13 14 QG 6 5 4 3 2

--- Contents ---

--- Introduction ---
It's a Jungle Out There

My granddad, D. H. Sykes, was thirty-eight years old when he volunteered to join the United States Army and go serve our country in World War II. He was the oldest man drafted in his unit. It never occurred to him to skip out on his responsibility as an American.

He felt the call of duty and he went to serve.

As a supply sergeant in Europe, Granddad didn't see any action, but "Old Doss" was appreciated because of his sense of duty, love of country, and most of all his love of freedom. "There are worse things than war," he said to me once. "What would *that* be, Granddad?" I asked. His reply: "When men lose their freedom."

Everything I saw him do was filled with integrity and a sense of true determination. He also had a twinkle in his eye and was a fantastic storyteller.

When he passed away in 1988, I received his *Basic Field Manual on Jungle Warfare* dated December 15, 1941. It became a treasured gift because it was his—but in a sense it was also a relic and seemed to have no practical use in my life—until recently. Thumbing through it again, I saw he had scrawled his name inside of it—and I became aware that he was dedicated to being prepared no matter what came his way. And then to serving how and where he was assigned.

As my job in field sales continued to get tougher, and as the economy tightened, I began to look for a way to toughen my own resolve and to exceed the sales goals that had been issued to me. I had opened Granddad's field manual just to reconnect with him; what I found was strong medicine for difficult situations.

As a Christian in sales, I try to be as tough as I can when I am out on the road and away from family . . . but it really is a jungle out there. We run the risk of being tripped up, wounded by the competition, and even killed spiritually if we give in to all the temptations we face on the road. The parallels are obvious: Stay fit. Keep your wits about you. Know your enemy. Serve your leader well. For those of us who are on the front lines in sales every day, it is tough, and we need a field manual as well.

I share this book as tribute to Granddad Sykes—and as tribute to the brave men and women who defend our country every day. They are the true warriors. We are privileged to work and live in a country where they stand in harm's way on our behalf; and they do it without hesitation.

Rules of Engagement

Here's my challenge to you: take the next twenty-two days and commit your sales to God. Consider it—five minutes each day to focus on how your life can improve under the leadership of Jesus Christ as your Commander and Chief.

I encourage you to study one day at a time and not tackle the book all at once. The format is simple. Each day you will do the following:

1. Read a verse.
2. Review your battle plan for the day.
3. Offer a prayer.
4. Record your thoughts.
5. Write down your prayer requests.

I believe there is no better manual for life than God's Word—but I hope this book will serve to encourage you to fight through the tough times and to come out alive and kicking on the other side of the jungle. God bless you.

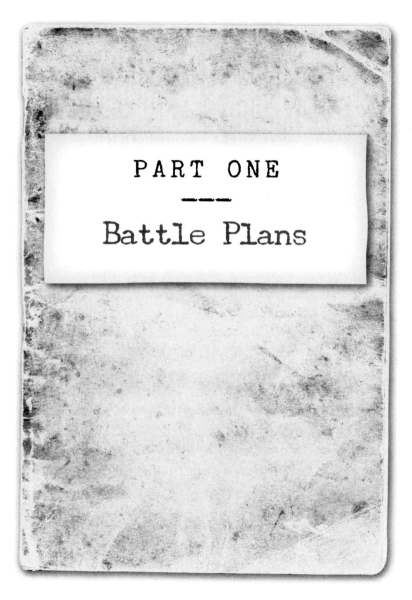

PART ONE

Battle Plans

- I am an American Soldier.
- I am a Warrior and a member of a team.
- I serve the people of the United States, and live the Army Values.
- I will always place the mission first.
- I will never accept defeat.
- I will never quit.
- I will never leave a fallen comrade.
- I am disciplined, physically and mentally tough, trained and proficient in my warrior tasks and drills.
- I always maintain my arms, my equipment, and myself.
- I am an expert and I am a professional.
- I stand ready to deploy, engage, and destroy the enemies of the United States of America in close combat.
- I am a guardian of freedom and the American way of life.
- I am an American Soldier.

You're in Enemy Territory

BASIC FIELD MANUAL

JUNGLE WARFARE
December 15, 1941

■ 1. GENERAL.—In jungle warfare the soldier fights two enemies: man and nature. Of the two, nature is often the more formidable. Troops newly arriving in tropical jungle areas experience a climate to which they are not accustomed and are exposed to diseases with which they are not familiar. These conditions impose a special responsibility on all commanders; they must assure themselves that their troops are adjusted to tropical climates and that the health and combat effectiveness of the command will insure the execution of the assigned mission under tropical jungle conditions.

Day One Verse

Even though I walk through the valley of the shadow of death, I will fear no evil, for you are with me; your rod and your staff, they comfort me.

Psalm 23:4

Day One Battle Plan

Inside the business jungle, every step you take may be booby-trapped by your competition or by the unseen hand of market forces. Even more interesting, you are also a Christian, or you are at least thinking about being one. Therefore, you also battle a deadly spiritual enemy who prowls around like a jungle cat wishing he could devour your soul. He and his commandos lie in wait, scheming and plotting about how they can throw anything in your path that will not only destroy your career but also your reputation, relationships, and rewards.

Uniquely, you are called to fight on both a business and a spiritual front simultaneously. It is important to understand that you can be attacked by dangerous enemies from many different sides. The terrain can be challenging, and the difficulties you may encounter can be exhausting. If you decide to go after your goals alone, it can mean you will be more susceptible to getting lost in the jungle.

You have a Guide you can call on. In fact, your Guide has

already won the battles you will be facing. As you step into enemy territory you will be asked to trust your Guide time and again.

You probably picked up this book (or received it as gift) because it said the word *Christian* on it. That word scares some people to death. All they can think of are those people who claim to be Christians and who run around acting like sanctimonious religious nuts getting into everybody's stuff.

Some people may ask (or you might have thought), "How can you be a sales superstar *and* be a Christian?" And some may also ask, "How can you be a soldier and be a Christian too?" Take a moment to reflect on those two questions.

I believe sales pros can be superstars and Christians.

What we do as salespeople creates jobs for people all over the world. Those jobs create income. That income provides food, clothing, and shelter. In addition, some people use that income to share with others who are less fortunate.

As for our revered United States military personnel, make no mistake, our brave, self-sacrificing men and women stand in front of those who would come to steal, kill, and destroy our way of life. This book honors their valor and service. In no way does it suggest that their exceptional commitment to our way of life and freedom is even remotely akin to the jobs we are asked to do in business. Theirs is the ultimate sacrifice, and we are able to perform our work because they stand in harm's way for us. God bless them with safety, and bring them home to us soon.

But we recognize that both sales pros and soldiers follow certain rules of engagement. The analogies are justified in the need for discipline, focused action, and determination. When military personnel break rank, go against protocol, or disobey orders, they are held accountable by military law. As sales professionals, when we are out of step with what our customers and our companies require of us, we can lose our jobs. As Christians we answer to God.

I think it is important on Day One in the jungle to establish the rules of engagement and to understand an important term:

Christian

Here's my definition of someone who follows Jesus Christ—see if you can sign up for following Christ through the jungle if this is what it means:

I believe Jesus is God's only Son and that He died for my sins. I cannot earn this freedom from my sins; it is a gift from God and is solely due to His grace and mercy.

I am commissioned to tell everyone that fact and to share it as the Good News.

I feel the presence of God's Holy Spirit as He leads me through the jungle in the presence of my enemies. When I go at it alone, I get lost. I start battling man, nature, and spirit—and I usually get into trouble. Because He loves me, God comes and finds me, binds my wounds, and we start over.

God believes that no man or woman should be left behind.

I believe He is right.

If you choose to take on the challenge of developing as a Christian *as well as* a salesperson, then your job will be harder, not easier. You will have to decide if you can muster the strength and the courage to press through the hardest of times and still retain your business integrity *and* the principles of your Christian faith while the rest of the world is going to hell all around you.

Yes, folks will take shots at you, *especially* if you are a Christian. Yes, you'll stumble and you'll be exhausted. Yes, you'll be ridiculed and persecuted—and when you receive your forecast and quota, I'm sure you'll feel tortured.

But you will also learn about a peace that passes all understanding. And you will find out how to navigate through the jungle with Someone who knows the way.

Day One Prayer

So, today on Day One, let's start this jungle trek with a prayer:

God, I can be a hardheaded, stubborn person, and I sometimes find myself lost in my own plans and schemes. Often, I let the company's plans drive me to the point of distraction and worry. I am coming to You to try and figure out how to make this job and my life better. I wake up and go to work. I lie down at night and I still feel like I am working. Often, I seldom see my family and I wonder if I am doing this for them or for some false sense of accomplishment. Right now, I am going to at least say, "You are smarter than I am." I am willing to reengage with You and to listen to You, God, as I make my way through this manual over the next twenty-two days. I will not quit on You, because I know You will not quit on me. Help me as I trust in You as my provision.

Name: _____ Date: _____

Title: _____ Your signature: _____

Day One: My Thoughts

When I read the verse for Day One, my
initial thoughts on Psalm 23:4 were:

_____

_____

_____

_____

_____

_____

How is God my provision?

_____

_____

_____

_____

_____

_____

Day One Prayer Requests

_____

_____

_____

_____

_____

The Sales Professional's Creed

BASIC FIELD MANUAL

■ l. Sleep off the ground to avoid dampness, reptiles, and especially insects. Climb a tree if mosquitoes and other insects are too bad near the ground.

■ m. If possible, travel with one or more companions.

■ n. Do not fear the jungle, for you should remember that if you keep relaxed and use your head you can live and travel alone for weeks in uninhabited country.

Day Two Verses

One of the teachers of the law came and heard them debating. Noticing that Jesus had given them a good answer, he asked him, "Of all the commandments, which is the most important?"

"The most important one," answered Jesus, "is this: 'Hear, O Israel, the Lord our God, the Lord is one. Love the Lord your God with all your heart and with all your soul and with all your mind and with all your strength.' The second is this: 'Love your neighbor as yourself.' There is no commandment greater than these."

Mark 12:28–31

Day Two Battle Plan

We began today's battle plan with a selection from Granddad's manual stating three edicts that can keep you alive in the jungle. They all suggest that if you are prepared, and you have a set of predetermined behaviors, you have nothing to fear.

Notice also that our Scripture verses suggest the same idea. They teach us that if we understand our commands, then we are safe to proceed through life. Jungle survival has at its very core a requirement that we have done our homework prior to the beginning of the battle.

Often, we are most at risk when we do not have a battle

plan. We are all cut from the same cloth—God knit our very souls with His own hands, and He stitched in a need for order and guidance.

Be aware, guidance can come from many voices. We must discern what wisdom really sounds like, and we must do it whether we are the best salesperson or the worst. No matter if you are at the top of the rankings or at the bottom of the heap, I have been where you are right now. I have celebrated onstage with my colleagues at the national sales meetings. And as I'm sure you can relate to, I've also sat outside of a customer's office with my face in my hands, wondering how I would ever hit my number.

Just like many of you, I have been laid off, rehired, promoted, transferred, restructured, retrained, downsized, supersized, marginalized, and, yes, even recognized.

Amidst it all God never changed. His commands remained constant.

It's easy to get sidetracked with life's ball of confusions, isn't it? I believe we find God when we are moved to rediscover what really matters in life. Then, we often find that God never left us—and no matter what we substituted for His love, we find out that what is most important to Him is *us*.

This book is not about being number one. Every other sales book you pick up will make you that promise. This book is about knowing *who* number one really is in your life and living your profession like you mean it.

These are tough times worldwide. Record layoffs. Economic

nightmares. Customers closing their doors. Product lines being discontinued. It's the news of the day; but it's not the Good News. As a Christian in sales, you have a higher calling.

On Day Two, consider what it means to have a personal creed. Take a moment to reread "The Soldier's Creed" in the front of this book; then return to this page. My son Mark shared it with me, and it is the current version of the Creed that was first published in the magazine *Infantry* on December 22, 2003.

As sales professionals who are also Christians I suggest that we also have a Creed. Consider these rules of engagement as you take on your life's calling—and feel free to rewrite them to fit your special areas of expertise and development:

- I am a Christian in sales.
- I am a sales warrior and a member of a team of professionals who count on me to be prepared.
- I serve a risen Savior, Jesus Christ; my customers; and my company with my best efforts.
- I will always place His mission for my life first.
- My family's needs are of the utmost importance and I will remain vigilant in my love for them.
- I will never accept defeat in the tasks my company has given me.
- My customers are counting on me.
- I will never quit on God because He never quits on

me. I frequently use prayer to communicate with my Commander, and I consistently ask for air cover.

- I will never leave a fallen comrade to wonder about heaven.
- I am spiritually disciplined, physically and mentally tough, trained, and proficient in my sales tasks.
- I always maintain my product and sales knowledge, and I strive daily to get better.
- I am an expert, and every day I can sell something to somebody.
- I stand ready to engage God and ask Him to destroy any and all spiritual enemies I may encounter in close combat.
- I will fight my competitors fairly but without tiring. I will not rest until my company's position is advanced.
- I am a guardian of sales wisdom and a purposeful way of life.
- I am a servant to my customers and my colleagues. I serve them with integrity and enthusiasm.
- I am a Christian in sales.

Day Two Prayer

Make a Commitment

If you are ready to dedicate your work to God, begin with this prayer, right now:

O merciful God, I come to You because You are the great I AM. My world is hectic and demanding. My fears often bring about dilemmas in my life that cause me to step up to a moral line and—as You know—to sometimes even cross it. I admit that I have taken control of the life You gave me. And now I want to give my life back to You, for I know that You are all-powerful, all-knowing, and all-caring. Sometimes I grow weary, and I need to know You are there for me—to comfort, guide, and direct me. Thank You for loving me. I'd like to share with You right now the things that are bothering me:

_____

_____

_____

_____

_____

_____

I accept Your leadership in my life today. I accept Jesus Christ as Lord and Savior of my life because I know that He is Your Son and gave His life for my sinfulness. I have reveled in building my own kingdom and tried to do it all by myself, but I admit that deep within me there is a gnawing and a hunger that I cannot satisfy. I ask to learn to hear Your voice before I speak, and I invite the indwelling of Your Holy Spirit into my life to encourage and guide me. God, I thank You that the work You have promised to do in me has already begun. Let my family, friends, coworkers, competitors, and customers see Your light in me.

In the name of Jesus Christ, I pray. Amen.

God is blessing you right now. Pause for a moment and be comfortable in His presence. You are a child of God, perfectly made to His specifications. God loves you, and you are important to Him. What you do from this day forth will sharpen your sales skills through a better understanding of your love for God. Let God love you. He never fails. He will never abandon you. His commands are perfect.

Day Two: My Thoughts

Based on prayer and the Holy Spirit, I would add this to "The Sales Professional's Creed":

How I can fulfill Jesus' commandment in
Mark 12 of giving God "all":

_____

_____

_____

_____

_____

_____

Day Two Prayer Requests

_____

_____

_____

_____

_____

_____

--- DAY THREE ---

Wild Hogs and Leeches!

BASIC FIELD MANUAL

■ 2. WILD HOGS.—Wild hogs are fearless and when in droves do not hesitate to attack man. The boars have needle sharp teeth which can inflict dangerous wounds. If a man is knocked down by the rush of these animals, they may gore or trample him to death. If unarmed men are attacked by a drove of wild hogs, it is best that they take to the trees.

■ 7. LEECHES.—a. *General.*—Land leeches occur in the jungles of South America. They are about 1 inch long, have slender bodies, and live in rain forests and rank jungle vegetation. They attach themselves readily and can penetrate a single thickness of cotton cloth. Their bites are pain-less but ulceration frequently follows.

b. *Treatment.*—Apply heat to the body of the leech and remove it. Apply iodine and a tight bandage to the wound.

Day Three Verses

Then Jesus said to his disciples: "Therefore I tell you, do not worry about your life, what you will eat; or about your body, what you will wear. Life is more than food, and the body more than clothes. Consider the ravens: They do not sow or reap, they have no storeroom or barn; yet God feeds them. And how much more valuable you are than birds! Who of you by worrying can add a single hour to his life? Since you cannot do this very little thing, why do you worry about the rest?"

Luke 12:22-26

Day Three Battle Plan

Wild hogs and leeches! For a moment, think about all the deadly animals a soldier might encounter, from snakes to spiders, to stinging insects.

For a couple of days, you have been thinking about the many enemies who are determined to kill your best sales and spiritual efforts. But have you considered that worry might be your greatest foe?

Go back and reread Jesus' words in the verses on page 20 *very thoughtfully*. Study each word.

Jesus deals with the heart of a Christian salesperson first. That's because He starts there with all of us no matter who we are or what we do. We are asked to examine our hearts and to see if they might be filled with worry.

As salespeople we are expected to drive the number, move the mountains, and make sure every customer on the planet has all the product they'll ever need! Our motivation *often* comes from worry about our jobs, the number, the quota.

But what happens when we aren't spinning our sunshine fast enough and our sales start to slip, our managers begin to frown, and our competitors dance around our failures like tigers at a barbecue?

Worry slips in on us. Doubt replaces confidence. Trophies become keenly important as they seem to be moving away from us. We press too hard sometimes, and we begin to substitute passion for our products with pressure on all those around us.

Or sometimes—we just check out.

As the WWII manual states, "Wild hogs are fearless and when in droves do not hesistate to attack man." Worry can come in droves as well, and it, too, does not hesitate to eat us alive.

Motivation is one thing, but worry is not healthy. Here's what Jesus puts at the top of the product brochure titled "Follow Me."

"Do not worry about your life."

Isn't worrying about your life sometimes a primary motivator?

Let me ask you something—be honest. Who is really the Lord of your life? Is it a person? A goal? Could it be your *job*?

We salespeople often say, "I have a family to feed, units to move, customers to satisfy." Yes, we do. But remember, we just learned that Jesus said, "Do not worry about your life." A few verses later, Jesus went on to say that if we seek God's kingdom, *He* will take care of our material needs (see verse 31). Be confident that God will do what He says He will do. Surely, Jesus did not leave the beauty and security of heaven to *lie* to us.

Believe what Jesus says: God will feed you because you are *valuable* to Him. Nowhere in the Bible does it say that God helps those who help themselves. First, you must realize this one truth:

Do not worry. God will provide.

So when you are particularly worried about your sales, keep this verse in your head so you can recite it to yourself and then do it: "*Cast all your anxiety on him because he cares for you*" (1 Peter 5:7). If you understand your true self-worth is built on God's love for you, you will be in a right place. You can then move with confidence in any situation and be focused on bringing effective solutions to your customers *regardless of any circumstances.*

Not convinced? Then, check out a guy named Paul who made and sold tents for a living and see if you've been through even half of what he went through:

> As God's fellow workers we urge you not to receive God's grace in vain. For he says,
>
> "In the time of my favor I heard you, and in the day of salvation I helped you." I tell you, now is the time of God's favor, now is the day of salvation.
>
> We put no stumbling block in anyone's path, so that our ministry will not be discredited. Rather, as servants of God we commend ourselves in every way: in great endurance; in troubles, hardships and distresses; in beatings, imprisonments and riots; in hard work, sleepless nights and hunger; in purity, understanding, patience and kindness; in the Holy Spirit and in sincere love; in truthful speech and in the power of God; with weapons of righteousness in the right hand and in the left; through glory and dishonor, bad report and good report; genuine, yet regarded as impostors; known, yet regarded as unknown; dying, and yet we live on; beaten, and yet not killed; sorrowful, yet always rejoicing; poor, yet making many rich; having nothing, and yet possessing everything. (2 Corinthians 6:1–10)

He suffered beatings. Imprisonment. Riots. Dishonor. Dying. Beatings (again)! It's sorrowful . . . and what does he say he uses in the midst of his jungle warfare . . . "weapons of righteousness in the right hand and in the left"!

Like Paul, we can then begin to say we

> have learned to be content whatever the circumstances. I know what it is to be in need, and I know what it is to have plenty. I have learned the secret of being content in any and every situation, whether well fed or hungry, whether living in plenty or in want. (Philippians 4:11–12)

Can you imagine the confidence that would radiate from you as you stood in front of your customers if they knew your faith was in something deeper than the sale?

Day Three Prayer

Dear God,

Thank You that I am valuable to You. I admit that sometimes I worry too much. In fact, sometimes I have worried myself to the point of distraction or poor performance. It is hard for me to trust You for all my needs. But You love me, and You will feed me. I'm not going to starve as long as I am in Your care. And I know that my basic needs as well as many other blessings are in store for me as I learn more about how valuable I am to You.

Jesus, thank You for loving me so much that You came to teach me. Let me learn to know You and love You better by studying and meditating slowly and with intention on Your words every day. I love You.

Amen.

Day Three: My Thoughts

What are my three to five biggest sales concerns?

For a moment, pretend Paul is your sales manager. Besides saying, "Don't worry," what else would he say to you?

Day Three Prayer Requests

_____

_____

_____

_____

_____

_____

Close Fighting

BASIC FIELD MANUAL

The Arms

■ 30. INFANTRY.—a. Jungle fighting is performed largely by infantry. Combat is usually characterized by close fighting. Support of infantry by other arms will frequently be impracticable or impossible.

b. Prior to the initiation of operations in jungle areas, a careful analysis of the terrain must be made to determine the practicability of transporting and employing the various organic infantry weapons within each area of operations. Based upon this analysis and the mission, task forces are organized so as to assure maximum tactical mobility and combat effectiveness.

Day Four Verses

Now a man came up to Jesus and asked, "Teacher, what good thing must I do to get eternal life?"

"Why do you ask me about what is good?" Jesus replied. "There is only One who is good. If you want to enter life, obey the commandments."

"Which ones?" the man inquired.

Jesus replied, "'Do not murder, do not commit adultery, do not steal, do not give false testimony, honor your father and mother,' and 'love your neighbor as yourself.'"

"All these I have kept," the young man said. "What do I still lack?"

Jesus answered, "If you want to be perfect, go, sell your possessions and give to the poor, and you will have treasure in heaven. Then come, follow me."

When the young man heard this, he went away sad, because he had great wealth.

Then Jesus said to his disciples, "I tell you the truth, it is hard for a rich man to enter the kingdom of heaven. Again I tell you, it is easier for a camel to go through the eye of a needle than for a rich man to enter the kingdom of God."

When the disciples heard this, they were greatly astonished and asked, "Who then can be saved?"

Jesus looked at them and said, "With man this is impossible, but with God all things are possible."

Matthew 19:16-26

Day Four Battle Plan

The Arms section from Granddad's *Basic Field Manual* lays out the truth very plainly. "Jungle fighting is performed largely by infantry. Combat is usually characterized by close fighting."

Every day when we go to work, it can feel like we are engaged in hand-to-hand combat with our competitors.

We are also engaged in heart-to-heart combat with the living God. Because we are tempted, because we can be greedy and selfish—we often end up at odds with the Master of the Universe . . . news flash: He's Bigger!

In today's verses, did you notice how close Jesus got to this guy's heart?

Yesterday we began to yield to God's enormous love for us by *allowing* Him to say, "I love you" and letting it break through the strongholds of our worries. As His Holy Spirit soothes our sales-focused souls, we begin to understand that we are destined for something greater than a year-end bonus or a glam trip to Cancún.

Those rewards are fabulous. Believe me, I take them when I earn them, and we all should. We work hard for them. But, in today's passage we are once again reminded that what matters to God is the Christian salesperson's heart. We are being called to look into our own priorities and see if they pass the Jesus test. I have to look into mine often, and sometimes

I come up sadly out of step. It is then that I realize I have replaced God's place in my life with a new priority.

This passage reminds us that "there is only One who is good." Thank heavens! That lets us off the hook of trying to be perfect. As long as we ask for forgiveness, turn away from our sin, and believe in Jesus Christ as our Savior, then our mistakes (past, present, and future) can be forgiven.

Don't let your fear of being discovered keep you at arm's length from God. God already knows what you have done and what you *will* do. You and I do not surprise Him. So stop rationalizing; God wants you to be honest with Him.

Think about this for a moment: before Jesus asked the rich young man His question, *Jesus knew ahead of time how the young man would answer.* The one thing this guy could not give up was his wealth, and that is why Jesus went in "jungle close" on him. Jesus was battling for the soul of this man.

Is He battling for your soul too?

Remember, God gave you the talents you have, your wealth, and the people you care about. But you cannot let *anything* come before your love of God, or He might choose to remove it to regain your focus on Him.

Each person's "wealth" can be different. It might be your house, car, professional title, your skills, your husband, your wife, your child, your membership. Can you see that the person, place, or thing already belongs to God? God is *sharing* it with you. It belongs to Him, and He has asked you to take care of it.

The next big question for your combat training is, what (or who) is sitting on the throne of your life? Is it any of the following?

- Another person
- Your job
- A grudge
- Lust
- Ambition
- Greed
- Family problems
- Your thirst for approval
- Your quest for possessions or success

You see, dear friend, wealth is neutral. But if you're possessive regarding it (or anything or anyone), it will eat you alive. You should multiply it to the best of your ability so that you can give it back to the One to whom it belongs.

Christian salesperson, you cannot serve both God and money.

Serve God. Earn money.

In fact, in the Bible, James (sounding like a grizzled, seasoned combat sergeant) issued this stern reprimand: "Submit yourselves to God" (James 4:7).

What causes fights and quarrels among you? Don't they come from your desires that battle within you?

You want something but don't get it. You kill and covet, but you cannot have what you want. You quarrel and fight. You do not have, because you do not ask God. When you ask, you do not receive, because you ask with wrong motives, that you may spend what you get on your pleasures.

You adulterous people, don't you know that friendship with the world is hatred toward God? Anyone who chooses to be a friend of the world becomes an enemy of God. Or do you think Scripture says without reason that the spirit he caused to live in us envies intensely? But he gives us more grace. That is why Scripture says:

"God opposes the proud but gives grace to the humble."

Submit yourselves, then, to God. Resist the devil, and he will flee from you. (James 4:1–7)

I could almost hear Louis Gossett Jr. playing the role of James, couldn't you?

How are you doing with God's gifts? What would happen if God asked you to surrender any of them to Him today as He asked Abraham to sacrifice his son Isaac, or the young rich young man to give up his wealth?

You are asked to be able to take care of all that has been given to you *and* to return it to its rightful Owner if He asks you to do so. When you are at ease in both of these roles, then you are ready for the Master to approach you closely on the battlefield. In fact, Jesus has a promise for you if you're willing to do this—He says in our Scripture that "you will have treasure in heaven" (Matthew 19:21).

Eternity is a long time to enjoy *that* treasure.

Day Four Prayer

Merciful God, I have wrapped myself in my wealth and the acquisition of it. Sometimes I am driven to keep all the balls in the air in my quest to succeed to the exclusion of all else. I have considered switching jobs for just a little more money, without seeking Your counsel, because I thought that would make me more secure. God, I confess that my trophies are very important to me. I realize that there are things, people, and projects that possess me. I am often out of balance and many times manipulative because I have my eyes only on the prize.

But You love me. God, You are so good. On the other hand, no matter how hard I try, I can never be good enough. But I can become more mature in my relationship with You and Your Son. Thank You that You press in close when I am in the fight of my life and You challenge me to turn my heart toward Your saving grace.

God, help me to take care of all that You have given me. In Jesus' name I pray. Amen.

Day Four: My Thoughts

One thing that is attached too closely to
my heart is:

_____

_____

_____

_____

_____

_____

I usually find my security in my . . .

_____

_____

_____

_____

_____

_____

Day Four Prayer Requests

_____

_____

_____

_____

_____

--- DAY FIVE ---

Use Your Compass

BASIC FIELD MANUAL

■ *b.* Never go anywhere without a compass, preferably a lensatic or prismatic compass, which you know how to use.

Day Five Verses

Now we see but a poor reflection as in a mirror; then we shall see face to face. Now I know in part; then I shall know fully, even as I am fully known.

And now these three remain: faith, hope and love. But the greatest of these is love.

1 Corinthians 13:12-13

Day Five Battle Plan

On Day Two, I told you that I have experienced high highs and low lows in sales. Why in the world would you want to learn from someone who was at the bottom of the sales list? Because, those of us who have failed and found our faith in the midst of it are best equipped to share our faults so that we might all learn together.

One glorious year, I had been at the top of my game, growing my territory and sales by more than $1 million and soaring with growth in excess of 160 percent. But by the next year, I found some of my customers to be tough to deal with, and a lack of new products combined with my own shortcomings all combined to make it hard for me to make the necessary adjustments.

I also know that many of us as salespeople can be a real pain to deal with too. I found myself acting out of character and sometimes standing on the edge of bargaining away my integrity just so that I could crawl back on top.

As a sales professional I had failed. As a Christian I had definitely lost my light.

At my lowest, God enabled me to recapture my passion for work, for Him, and for my own goals. He built a flame inside of me that drove me to help train others, to humble myself and know that God is in control. All I want today is for people to say, "There goes Chris Cunningham, a salesperson after God's own heart."

I was so thankful that God knew me—and loved me anyway.

God knows you—and loves you, too—completely. And His love is a wonderful, unyielding, unwavering, unconditional, unselfish, and uncanny love that the Greeks called *agape*. It is best characterized by its unconditional and sacrificial nature.

In the sales jungle, His unconditional love is our compass. When all else fails, it always points us in the right direction. He always welcomes home His prodigals. Always.

Let me ask you a question: What will you do the first day of your eternity, when you stand before God and are captivated by His presence? For the first time in your life, you will be able to see your Maker wonderfully and clearly—you will *feel* how much you are loved.

But is it possible that you could be able to break through the dimness of this world to experience the true reality of an overwhelming *agape* love even today?

The answer is *yes*! We can catch crystal clear glimpses of it today—if we are looking for it.

We scratch out an existence all our lives, dimly seeing flashes of God's eternal love in our hearts' peripheral vision. Occasionally, we even give in to the soft voice of the Holy Spirit, which calls to us and woos us. But all too often we're too preoccupied with our mundane daily lives to notice the subtlety of God's love.

But on that day when we meet Him in eternity, there will be nothing to hide behind—no more excuses. We will be totally and completely exposed.

And loved—*agape*!

With nothing between us and God, we will feel the full force of His love for us as we never have before. Like newborn babies, we will look upward and see the wonderful, awe-inspiring, indescribable, and perfect face of our Creator for the first time. We will be in the presence of a love so pure that it will utterly consume us. Not since our time in the womb will we have ever experienced anything so symbiotic.

In today's verses, the apostle Paul concluded that there are three great things we can practice in order to be ready for that day: faith, hope, and love. But the greatest of these is love. If we begin the practice of giving and receiving unconditional love today, God's love for us will not seem so difficult to discern when we see it during our lives on earth.

Today I'd like you to make a pledge to begin loving others as God loves you. Followers of Christ always have a true compass. It is combat ready: unyielding, unwavering, unconditional, unselfish, and uncanny.

Day Five Prayer

Dear God,

Your Word says, "Love never fails." You are Love. So I know You will never fail to love me. I am on Your radar. My face is on the face of Your compass. And I am learning that Your face should be on mine.

I know that if I don't have love, I have nothing. God, all my professional life, I have been taught to gain; it is how I have been trained. Oh, God, I want You to train me to gain in my capacity to love and be loved. I want to gain Your favor and a better understanding of Your love. Teach me Your ways and help me to understand what love truly is.

Lord, please make me patient; then make me kind. Stop me from envying others. Help me not to boast. Stop me before my pride gets the best of me. Tame my rudeness before it starts. Purge my selfishness. Temper me, so I'm not so easily angered. Let me keep no record of others' wrongs. Keep me away from evil, and keep evil away from me. Let me be excited about telling the truth. Help me to protect what is true, to hope without failing, and to persevere without wavering.

Sometimes I act like a spoiled child. Help me, instead, to act like a well-trained soldier and to trust that You will serve as my compass in life. And let me see You and Your Son, Jesus, in whose precious name I pray, clearly today. Finally, help me never fail to share Your love.

I love You, God. Thank You for loving me with a wild and unwavering love.

Amen.

Day Five: My Thoughts

Has anyone shown you unconditional love?
If so, describe what they did for you? If
not, describe why God would give you such
a gift.

_____

_____

_____

_____

_____

_____

Name the people to whom you will start
showing love first and how you will do it.

_____

_____

_____

_____

_____

_____

Day Five Prayer Requests

_____

_____

_____

_____

_____

_____

--- DAY SIX ---

Take Refuge

Day Six Verses

O LORD my God, I take refuge in you; save and deliver me from all who pursue me, or they will tear me like a lion and rip me to pieces with no one to rescue me.

Psalm 7:1-2

The LORD is a refuge for the oppressed, a stronghold in times of trouble.

Psalm 9:9

Turn your ear to me, come quickly to my rescue; be my rock of refuge, a strong fortress to save me.

Psalm 31:2

Day Six Battle Plan

Are the pressures of life pursuing you? Do you have a fierce competitor who, like a lion, would like to rip you to pieces? Are you battling against a difficult quota, an unreachable forecast, an unrelenting boss, a saturated market, an inferior product line, or an oversized territory? Is your company experiencing massive layoffs or government bailouts that make you doubt the security of your future?

What topics do you and your spouse and/or friends talk about when you consider the financial instability of the world economy?

Who do you believe is really in control?

Does your editorial and political conversation match your prayers to God?

Take a look at each psalm in its context.

David, a warrior like you, was *singing* these psalms with great power. In the first passage, our main verse for today, he was literally crying out to God against another warrior, named Cush, who had been sent to kill him. In this psalm, David first of all sang out, "O LORD my God!"

Then he made an incredible statement of faith—"I take refuge in You." Finally, we see that David made a request that you can make today too: "Save and deliver me from *all* who pursue me." This prayer provides an example of David's immediate and very vocal movement *toward God* to solve his problems.

David was not beating around the bush or treading lightly into God's presence. He was afraid and needed God's immediate help. But instead of remaining fearful, David boldly and expectantly approached God with his needs. At the end of this psalm (7:17), David resolved to give thanks to the Lord because of God's righteousness, and to sing praise to the Lord Most High!

This prayer makes me think of the former Los Angeles Dodgers pitcher/Major League Baseball MVP Orel Hershiser (one of my heroes). During the final game of the World Series, the camera panned across the field into the dugout to show the world Orel's faith in action. *He was singing praises to God during the game!* He later sang the same song of praise (the Doxology) again on the *Tonight Show* with Johnny Carson. And my beloved Dodgers went on to win the 1988 World Series!

In your quiet time this week—in your car, on the train, in the shower, somewhere—I challenge you to *sing out loud* to God. Tell God about your fears, and then ask Him to save and deliver you. God will respond to that request! He will provide a refuge for you as you try to navigate through the difficulties of your job, as you try to discern what turn the world will take, as you hope for your own business to succeed.

Often when I am in the sales jungle, I find myself humming the words from one of the great hymns of the Christian faith. Their boldness, directness, and clarity are a welcome reminder that "if God is for me, who can be against me" and they bolster my confidence and resolve.

In fact, they provide a perfect refuge for us as we recharge our spiritual batteries:

"A mighty fortress is our God. A bulwark never failing; our helper he amid the flood of mortal ills prevailing."

"A Mighty Fortress Is Our God": Google this great hymn when you have some time. It reminds us that we are in a daily battle not only against our competition, but also against an evil force . . . and it reminds us of Psalm 46:1, that "God is our refuge and strength, an ever-present help in trouble."

Day Six Prayer

Praise God from Whom all blessings flow;
Praise Him, all creatures here below;
Praise Him above, ye heavenly host;
Praise Father, Son, and Holy Ghost.

(The Doxology,
Thomas Ken, 1674)

Day Six: My Thoughts

List the times that God has been your refuge in the last six months.

_____

_____

_____

_____

_____

_____

_____

List at least two current circumstances in which you need God's protection. Now commit them to God with confidence that He will be your refuge in these troubles just as He did for others in times past.

_____

_____

_____

_____

_____

_____

_____

Day Six Prayer Requests

Open the Lines
of Communication

BASIC FIELD MANUAL

SIGNAL COMMUNICATION

■ 92. CARE OF SIGNAL EQUIPMENT.—The care of signal equipment is of great importance, especially in the rainy season. Prior to beginning jungle operations, every possible measure should be taken to dry out and then protect equipment.

Day Seven Verses

We can make our own plans, but the LORD gives the right answer. People may be pure in their own eyes, but the LORD examines their motives. Commit your actions to the LORD, and your plans will succeed. The LORD has made everything for his own purposes, even the wicked for a day of disaster. The LORD detests the proud; they will surely be punished. Unfailing love and faithfulness make atonement for sin. By fearing the LORD, people avoid evil. When people's lives please the Lord, even their enemies are at peace with them. Better to have little, with godliness, than to be rich and dishonest. We can make our plans, but the LORD determines our steps.

Proverbs 16:1-9 NLT

Day Seven Battle Plan

Who helps you prepare your steps?

Have you prayed to God for help with your sales? Your customers? Your family? Sometimes it is hard to know what to pray for, but God loves it when you talk to Him. He loves the sound of your voice—God loves to hear from you because He is a loving Father.

Proverbs 16:3 tells us to commit whatever we do to the Lord and our plans will succeed. It almost sounds like a blank check, doesn't it? However, before you pray for your sales plan and commit it to God, make sure you have first committed *yourself* to Him.

We are to always be growing in our likeness to God, so when we examine our motives, we need to hold them up to the standard of His character. For a better understanding of how to judge your requests to God, try this little test:

- Will the issue you are praying about lead you toward truth?
- Is it pure?
- Is it loving?
- Is it kind?

If the answer to all four questions is yes, then know that your prayer request fits with the pattern God demonstrates to us in His Word. You can bet He'll answer your request. If it doesn't line up with the standards of His Word, then know that God will not do something that goes against His nature, which is holy.

Remember, *God's love and faithfulness to you never go away*. In fact, God's Son, Jesus Christ, loved you so much that He covered your sins by dying on the cross, and then He rose from the dead. There is not another faith on earth that claims such a wonderful claim. "God is my strong salvation; what foe have I to fear?" says the hymn.

So God, in His wisdom, provided a way—even when *you* can't figure out how to be true, pure, loving, and kind—for you to get right with Him through His Son and then daily accept His forgiveness.

I'd like to issue you a challenge for today: turn away from your mistakes and sins in repentance, learn from them, and ask God to move you toward love and faithfulness instead. Let it start today. When you begin to do that, you begin to practice your faith and to have a two-way relationship with the God of the universe. The changes that will happen next are incredible. God will start to *commune* with you.

When you are in communion with God, you can really share your plans with Him, because you will be relying on His instruction instead of your own wants. The great I AM will begin to teach you what really matters in life and to lift your soul's heavy burdens. As you commune with God, your plans will be born in an atmosphere of His character. You may even find that you are learning to hear God's direction and that God's plan is better than your plan. Then, when you ask Him to bless you, He will do so gladly because you are committed to Him first.

You'll notice from Granddad's field manual that we are reminded that care of your "signal equipment," especially when it is rainy, is a priority for the soldier who has been dropped into battle in the jungle. As Christians, our signal equipment—our means of hearing God's direction—is the fact that we have the Holy Spirit living inside of us. Regardless of the storms we go through, we are called to take heed of His voice and to recognize its unique pitch and cadence.

Finally, in today's Scripture passage, we read about another clue as to how to approach God with our plans: avoid evil by fearing God.

The fear of the Lord is the reverent knowledge that God is holy. When you realize this sacred truth, you will do anything you can to make sure that your actions, your business plans, and your life all reflect this insight. You will find that you "fear" being outside of God's presence and approval. We must desire to be in Christ when we make decisions so God doesn't have to call our motives into account. God has an exciting plan! So commune with God, obey His simple directions, and commit your plans to Him. Then your plans will succeed.

Day Seven Prayer

Dear God,

Thank You for Your holy presence. Through prayer, I know what it feels like to be in communion with You—it's powerful, awe inspiring, and loving. Help me to stay in this special presence when I am building my sales plans, when I am talking to my customers, and when I am living my life.

Lord, thank You for sharing Your plan with me. I love You, God—thank You for forgiving me and helping me to put You first. Amen.

Day Seven: My Thoughts

List a few times when you did not commit your plans to God first. What did you learn?

Does God have a plan He wants you to commit to today? Ask Him:

_____

_____

_____

_____

_____

_____

Day Seven Prayer Requests

_____

_____

_____

_____

_____

_____

--- DAY EIGHT ---

The Battle Is
for Your Soul

BASIC FIELD MANUAL

POISONOUS JUNGLE SNAKES

■ *b. Viperine snakes.*—Local symptoms are marked at the site of the bite—pain, oozing of blood and serum, and thrombosis (clotting of blood in veins), followed by gangrene. Death occurs in one of the following ways:

■ (1) Immediately, from thrombosis, if the poison is injected into a vein or a large dose is given.

■ (2) In a few hours, due to heart failure from paralysis of the brain centers.

■ (3) In a few days, from secondary bleeding due to the action of the poison in preventing blood clotting.

■ (4) From secondary infection of the gangre-nous area at the site of the bite.

Day Eight Verses

So the LORD God said to the serpent, "Because you have done this, cursed are you above all the livestock and all the wild animals! You will crawl on your belly and you will eat dust all the days of your life. And I will put enmity between you and the woman, and between your offspring and hers; he will crush your head, and you will strike his heel."

Genesis 3:14,15

Day Eight Battle Plan

From the beginning of time, there has been a war for our souls.

In God's original plan, there has always been a need for a Savior. In John 3 we read: "In the *beginning* was the Word, and the Word was with God, and the Word was God. *He was with God in the beginning*" (emphasis added).

God set forth the original battle plan, and within that plan one angel named Lucifer broke rank. He believed he was supposed to be the Commander in Chief, and when God explained the way it really was (and is), he rebelled and took one-third of the soldiers with him.

Then he began the implementation of what he thought would be the ultimate in jungle warfare: "If I can't win the battle of heaven," he plotted, "then I'll infiltrate the rest of the Lord's army, His precious creation!"

Relentlessly he devises and crafts situations that will prevent many from ever believing in the living God. We are not able to stand alone against the wiles of the devil. Our only hope is that God will come and ask us to join Him in His battalion.

For those of us who have answered that call and are now known as believers, the enemy relentlessly attacks without provocation. He shows up late at night in a hotel room, in a harmless business lunch, on an expense report, in a church positioning statement we let slide, at a national sales meeting—always where we least expect it.

Do you remember that Eve seemed to have no fear of the serpent? Wonder why? I believe it was because the world had not yet fallen.

What about us? We are too naive sometimes to even recognize the destruction slithering our way, aren't we? And then, as we become more cavalier, we even find ourselves seeking out the serpent.

"Where are you?" That was God's first question to man and woman. It came after their encounter with the serpent.

Wow! We know that God knew where they were—so why did He ask them this question?

So that they could . . . confess their sins.

"Where are you, Christian salesperson?" God asks the same question of us, doesn't He?

After Adam and Eve ate the apple, notice what happened as the garden of life and its perfect promise of constant communion with God became a jungle filled with warfare and destruction: God moved in to protect His people, and He made a promise.

Just for the record, God *never* makes a promise He can't keep. My pastor taught me that throughout the Bible, we see time and time again, God continued to provide a way for there to be a Savior for all mankind. In Genesis, God called Him a "headcrusher" who would take out the evil, rebellious snake.

Throughout history, God's opposition and enemies have put into motion their own evil plans . . . often hell-bent on destroying God's people. These were insidious plans they believed would destroy the lineage that would produce a Savior, who would crush evil. And time and time again God poured out His mercy and safe passage so that one day Messiah would be born. Think about it: an ark that saved a family from a worldwide flood; a baby named Moses in a small basket floating down the river, rescued by a royal woman; an old man and woman who had a baby at an unthinkable age; a shepherd boy who would become king and escape death in battle, time and again; and a Messiah baby born miraculously and saved even under the murderous reign of a tyrant named Herod.

God always keeps His promises. Even in the middle of jungle warfare. Especially when we think that we can take no more of the difficulty of surviving in a hostile environment.

Did you see the movie *The Passion of the Christ*? If so, do you remember the scene where Jesus is praying in the Garden of Gethsemane, and the blood is dripping like sweat from His head? Slinking around behind Him, cowering and plotting in the shadows, was Satan. Suddenly Christ stands and "crushes the head of a snake." It was awesome!

"The battle is mine!" says the Lord.

Rest assured, on Good Friday, when the jungle looked darker than ever before, the world and the Old Snake thought they had won the battle and that somehow, after thousands of years, God had broken His first promise. Not a chance!

When God reached into that tomb and pulled His boy up into heaven, it was the end for the devil. The curtain in the temple tore because at that split second we no longer needed a priest to pray on our behalf—we could enter the temple because Jesus became the High Priest and Advocate for us in heaven!

One day you may find yourself in your own dark moment,

one where you are terrified and wonder how you could ever have been so stupid to have allowed yourself to engage the enemy in such a dangerous fashion. Better to avoid the snakes in the jungle. Ask Jesus, the "headcrusher" to stomp out the perils that are both seen and unseen. Trust Him. Nothing can separate you from His love—not even snakebites.

Day Eight Prayer

Dear God,

I come to You today to begin anew. I confess to You that I have allowed myself to be snakebitten. Whether it was in my attitude or my actions with customers, employers, or family, I have listened to the whispers of darkness instead of renewing my soul under Your care.

As I go through my day today, give me eyes to see through the thicket and ears to hear Your direction. Let me not confuse beauty with blessing as I am keenly aware that sometimes the most beautiful things are the most evil. Give me a heart for living dangerously as a servant who would dare to tell the world about what You have done for me.

Thank You, God, that from the beginning You have prepared a battle plan that cannot fail. Thank You that I love You only because through Your mercy and grace, You came and found me in the jungle and You first loved me! Amen.

Day Eight: My Thoughts

I hunger for my heart to beat cleanly and
without poison. Lord, hear my confession
as I turn away from temptation:

_____

_____

_____

_____

_____

_____

Today I am going to commit the following
to God:

_____

_____

_____

_____

_____

_____

Day Eight Prayer Requests

Fit to Command

BASIC FIELD MANUAL

■ 8. PHYSICAL CONDITIONING.—The hardships of jungle operations demand physical fitness and acclimation of individuals. The loss of body fluids due to perspiration, the increased concentration of the blood plasma and urine, the elevation of body temperature due to physical exertion at high external temperatures, the effects of the sun, and the cooling of the body surfaces by the relatively cool winds at night all tend to lower the resistance of the body. Unless the physical condition of a command is excellent, many casualties will result.

Day Nine Verses

I love you, O LORD, my strength. The LORD is my rock, my fortress and my deliverer; my God is my rock, in whom I take refuge. He is my shield and the horn of my salvation, my stronghold. I call to the LORD, who is worthy of praise, and I am saved from my enemies. The cords of death entangled me; the torrents of destruction overwhelmed me. The cords of the grave coiled around me; the snares of death confronted me. In my distress I called to the LORD; I cried to my God for help. From his temple he heard my voice; my cry came before him, into his ears.

Psalm 18:1-6

He reached down from heaven and rescued me; he drew me out of deep waters. He rescued me from my powerful enemies, from those who hated me and were too strong for me. They attacked me at a moment when I was in distress, but the LORD supported me. He led me to a place of safety; he rescued me because he delights in me . . . The LORD rewarded me for doing right. He has seen my innocence.

Psalm 18:16-19,24 NLT

Day Nine Battle Plan

You have now been pursuing God for more than a week through this devotional. If you began this on a Sunday, I pray that your position affords you this as a day of rest, as your Sabbath. Yet even if it doesn't, and you must work, I believe today's meditation will help you through your day.

Today, let's focus on God's faithfulness and on your physical fitness.

First, take a moment to reread the Scriptures and notice how faithful God is! Today's passages teach that God both listens *and* responds to you. But look at the reason God does these things. In verse 19, it says He does them because *you delight Him.*

Let's do a little spiritual exercise. Pause. Now, close your eyes and imagine God's love radiating all around you like sunshine. This is your first exercise in being still before the Lord—feeling His love.

Stop reading for just a moment and think on this for a couple of minutes:

You delight God.

I know this made you smile. It always makes me smile, and as Will Ferrell said as Buddy in *Elf*, "smiling is my favorite."

Did you feel how God's love warms your soul as basking in the sun does your skin? It washes over you and bathes you in joy. Did you feel the delight the Lord finds in you? God loves you so much! It should put a smile on your face, because this is your destiny!

Chris, smiling? Really. What does smiling have to do with jungle warfare?

My friend, the rules of surviving in this jungle are much different than the rules of any other kind of warfare. You must condition yourself to be able to recognize how much you are loved by God. This will give you the confidence you need to be able to stay on track and complete the work of your day. Your smile is an outward and visible sign of God's incredible power that is alive inside of you. Don't hide that light under a bushel!

Now, here's some tough jungle language for you:

Your physical health is a direct reflection of whether or not you believe God is really living inside of you. Have you ever heard it said that your body is a living temple?

You know the joke about the lady in church who complained to the preacher, "Preacher, the teenagers are chewing gum in the church!" And the wise old preacher thought for a moment and said, "Madam, the churches are chewing gum."

Please—make a commitment to begin to think of your body (and mind) as God's holy temple.

```
Start small. Take five minutes right now
and write down two food and beverage
choices you are going to bring under
```

control. Make a change, soldier! Ask God
to help you!

Now push yourself just a little bit.
What exercise will you do twice this
week, and can you commit to *doing it
just twice* weekly for of the rest of
your life?

The workweek will bring its own cares—the highs and lows
of our profession, the rivalry of the competition, the crowded
marketplace, and the weariness of travel and separation from
your loved ones. But right now, wherever you are, take heart,
because you delight the God of the entire universe! Make a

commitment to improve your mind and body in a way that thanks Him for living in you.

The realization that God created you and that He *delights in you* will help you as you enjoy your friends and family. Let that one thought dwell in you through your day and give you supernatural energy for whatever you may be doing or might face during the coming week.

Day Nine Prayer

Dear God,

You are the mighty, one-and-only God! I'm fired up that You delight in me! Thank You! Let me be worthy of that delight today.

Grant me a steady mind, an honest heart, a strong body, a true tongue, and a boldness to approach my customers with You in my heart. If I am not clean, and if I am not in Your will, then nudge me back into Your delight.

Help me to be able to pray like the person who wrote Psalm 18, and let me use that prayer as my guide today. Keep me in Your presence, Lord, and continually draw me close to You.

Help me to see Your delight in others and to bring Your light to them.

In Jesus' name I pray. Amen.

Day Nine: My Thoughts

List some things you do that delight God:

_____

_____

_____

_____

_____

_____

Today I am going to commit the following to God:

_____

_____

_____

_____

_____

Day Nine Prayer Requests

_____

_____

_____

_____

_____

_____

Safe Rations: Living Water

BASIC FIELD MANUAL

■ *f.* Running water is usually purer than still water, but all drinking water should be boiled or chlorinated. (See ch. 2.) Most mud or other solids in water can be removed by straining the water through a cloth or by stirring a small amount of alum into the water to cause the solids to settle.

■ *g.* If lost, remember that if a man goes down slope he will come to a stream, and that watercourses, besides furnishing a means of travel and a supply of water and food, almost always lead to inhabited valleys or costal [*sic*] regions.

Day Ten Verses

The Pharisees heard that Jesus was gaining and baptizing more disciples than John, although in fact it was not Jesus who baptized, but his disciples. When the Lord learned of this, he left Judea and went back once more to Galilee.

Now he had to go through Samaria. So he came to a town in Samaria called Sychar, near the plot of ground Jacob had given to his son Joseph. Jacob's well was there, and Jesus, tired as he was from the journey, sat down by the well. It was about the sixth hour.

When a Samaritan woman came to draw water, Jesus said to her, "Will you give me a drink?" (His disciples had gone into the town to buy food.)

The Samaritan woman said to him, "You are a Jew and I am a Samaritan woman. How can you ask me for a drink?" (For Jews do not associate with Samaritans.)

Jesus answered her, "If you knew the gift of God and who it is that asks you for a drink, you would have asked him and he would have given you living water."

"Sir," the woman said, "you have nothing to draw with and the well is deep. Where can you get this living water? Are you greater than our father Jacob, who gave us the well and drank from it himself, as did also his sons and his flocks and herds?"

Jesus answered, "Everyone who drinks this water will be thirsty again, but whoever drinks the water I give him will never thirst. Indeed, the water I give him will become in him a spring of water welling up to eternal life."

The woman said to him, "Sir, give me this water so that I won't get thirsty and have to keep coming here to draw water."

He told her, "Go, call your husband and come back."

"I have no husband," she replied.

Jesus said to her, "You are right when you say you have no husband. The fact is, you have had five husbands, and the man you now have is not your husband. What you have just said is quite true."

"Sir," the woman said, "I can see that you are a prophet. Our fathers worshiped on this mountain, but you Jews claim that the place where we must worship is in Jerusalem."

Jesus declared, "Believe me, woman, a time is coming when you will worship the Father neither on this mountain nor in Jerusalem. You Samaritans worship what you do not know; we worship what we do know, for salvation is from the Jews. Yet a time is coming and has now come when the true worshipers will worship the Father in spirit and truth, for they are the kind of worshipers the Father seeks. God is spirit, and his worshipers must worship in spirit and in truth."

The woman said, "I know that Messiah" (called Christ)

"is coming. When he comes, he will explain everything to us."

Then Jesus declared, "I who speak to you am he."

John 4:1-26

As the deer pants for streams of water, so my soul pants for you, O God. My soul thirsts for God, for the living God.

Psalm 42:1-2

Day Ten Battle Plan

In sales, you no doubt find yourself in compromising situations daily and circumstances that vie for your attention constantly—just as the Samaritan woman at the well did. Like her, you may thirst and seek to quench your desire with many things, but only Jesus Christ, the Living Water, can quench a thirsty soul.

A deer will not come out of hiding if it believes danger is nearby. It will wait, biding its time until it is sure it's safe to come out. When it does, during the heat of the day, can you imagine how good the cold water of a fresh, flowing stream must taste?

As you face the dangers of your profession and the possible loss of your integrity, you must also flee from the danger and seek God to not only quench your thirst but to protect you—put your hope in the Lord. When you arrive in God's presence, realize that He is rejuvenating you and refueling you so that you can carry on through the jungle. Only there at His base camp are you truly safe.

In taking steps to seek Him out, such as following this manual, you have shown that you hunger and thirst for God. As you seek Him, He guarantees that you will find Him. His overwhelming peace and love will break through the tangled vines and unseen trappings of your everyday life. In order to win the battle over the stress of your job, you must learn to rest and relax in His presence.

Carry Living Water in your canteen as you go through your day; drink from the overflowing cup of *Christ's presence* even while you are working. Communion with Him doesn't just have to be for times of meditation and quiet. Your customers will notice the Spirit of God that is inside of and all around you—and they, too, will begin to thirst for Living Water.

Day Ten Prayer

Dear God,

I am so thirsty for Your presence. Sometimes I am afraid, lost, pursued, or confused—I'm in hiding, waiting to drink of Your wisdom and direction. Be Living Water for my soul today. Lord, You know I pant for success, but I desire to long for Your love and approval above any reward of men. Lord, help me to run to You to satisfy my thirsts, and not any substitute of the world.

Let me take my panting for success and turn it into a lapping up of Your love. Let me rush into Your presence and protection quickly, at the first sign of temptation or danger— and let me never delay, lest the roaring lion devour me.

I know I cannot do it all by myself, but I can do all things through Christ who strengthens me. Satisfy my thirst for You, God. Let me swim in the refreshing pool of Your love. Amen.

Day Ten: My Thoughts

In John 4:1-26, I learned that the Samaritan woman tried to satisfy her thirst with:

_____

_____

_____

_____

_____

_____

I have tried satisfying my thirst with:

_____

_____

_____

_____

_____

_____

Day Ten Prayer Requests

--- DAY ELEVEN ---

Trust the Higher Commander

BASIC FIELD MANUAL

■ (2) Since combat in the jungle will ordinarily develop into numerous small independent actions, the initiative and troop-leading ability of lower commanders are of major importance. Having been given the objective of the force as well as its own objective, and knowing the intention of the higher commander, each lower unit must consider itself as a self-contained unit with a definite task to accomplish, without expectation of direct assistance from adjacent units.

Day Eleven Verses

"Do not let your hearts be troubled. Trust in God; trust also in me. In my Father's house are many rooms; if it were

not so, I would have told you. I am going there to prepare
a place for you. And if I go and prepare a place for you, I
will come back and take you to be with me that you also
may be where I am. You know the way to the place where
I am going." Thomas said to him, "Lord, we don't know
where you are going, so how can we know the way?" Jesus
answered, "I am the way and the truth and the life. No one
comes to the Father except through me. If you really knew
me, you would know my Father as well. From now on, you
do know him and have seen him."

John 14:1-7

Day Eleven Battle Plan

How many times have you heard the phrase "Failing to plan
is planning to fail"? If we run after our sales opportunities in
a haphazard, nonstrategic way, we often end up scattered and
ineffective, don't we?

As a Christian in sales, consider for a moment the ultimate
strategy of God the Father. Even before time was recorded,
God had a no-fail plan to redeem us through Jesus and His
life-giving sacrifice at a perfect moment in time.

God also knew your heart at that very moment. The depth
of that incredible, powerful insight should provide a strength
to your walk with Christ that emboldens you to step out into
your job with great confidence and courage.

In this battle of Jungle Warfare, God has done all of the reconnaissance.

The ultimate strategy is to love God with all of our hearts, minds, and souls—and to know that our purpose on earth is to honor Him, not to try to stack the deck in our own favor, but rather to be humble in His presence.

Once we realize that truth, we are free to rely on God's eternal provision to set our minds and sales strategies within the context of eternal thinking.

Your freedom rests in God's plan.

Jesus is the ultimate Scout. He has gone ahead to heaven to prepare a place for us. When the disciples asked Him about how to get there, Jesus told them simply that *He* was the way—*the* way, *the* truth, and *the* life. The only way to the Father is through the Son.

In Granddad's *Basic Field Manual* it says, "Carefully selected guides whose loyalty and integrity are unquestioned should be secured prior to the beginning of operations." It also says, "The use of native troops, organized and controlled by the commander of the expeditionary force, not only will help to lessen any objection to the presence of our forces, but will strengthen solidarity against a common enemy."

God's brilliant, flawless plan once again is revealed, and His victory is already assured. Prior to time, He carefully selected Jesus, whose loyalty and integrity are unquestioned! When we stand under His command, we are with a native of heaven, someone who speaks the local language. Even better, He also walked this earth and knows about our pain and difficulties. Through His guidance we are able to defeat a common enemy!

Day Eleven Prayer

Dear God,

Thank You for sending Your Son, Jesus. Thank You for seeing me through His righteousness and not condemning me to death for my sins! Thank You, God, for Your grace!

Lord, let me see Jesus in my actions and choices. Let me reflect the deep change that Your grace permits in my life as I grow more and more like You. When I am working today, let me see Jesus in others, and let them see Jesus in me.

God, help me to share You with those I encounter, that they, too, can meet Your Son and become right with You through Christ. As I look at Your people, help me to see them as more than a sale, a number, a target, or a goal. Help me to see each as a child of God and a soul that is longing for You. Show me how I can help them.

In the name of Jesus I pray. Amen.

Day Eleven: My Thoughts

How familiar are you with Jesus' plans?
List three things you believe He says
are non-negotiables when you are
following Him.

_____

_____

_____

_____

_____

_____

Ask God for some practical ways you might
avoid the snares of the enemy. What do
you think He is telling you to do?

_____

_____

_____

_____

_____

_____

Day Eleven Prayer Requests

--- DAY TWELVE ---

Disciplined Deliverance

Day Twelve Verses

Jesus answered them, "It is not the healthy who need a doctor, but the sick. I have not come to call the righteous, but sinners to repentance."

Luke 5:31-32

Therefore, there is now no condemnation for those who are in Christ Jesus, because through Christ Jesus the law

of the Spirit of life set me free from the law of sin and
death.

Romans 8:1–2

Day Twelve Battle Plan

Are you a conscript under God's perfect command?

When God calls you to join His ranks, what must you do?
Repent.

Disciplined deliverance is a formula. Discipline yourself
to repentance, and God through His mercy will deliver you.
What does repent mean? Turn from your selfishness and put
all of your trust in God. When you accept Jesus into your
heart as your personal Lord and Savior, you become His—the
Father gives you to Him. You then decide to discipline your life
according to Scripture.

Jesus opens the way to heaven for us. There is not one thing
we can do ourselves to get into heaven. Take a moment and
read Revelation 3:19–22; it's interesting to see what it's like
belonging to Jesus and being under His disciplined leadership!

Those whom I love I rebuke and discipline. So be earnest,
and repent. Here I am! I stand at the door and knock. If
anyone hears my voice and opens the door, I will come in
and eat with him, and he with me. To him who overcomes,
I will give the right to sit with me on my throne, just as I

overcame and sat down with my Father on his throne. He who has an ear, let him hear what the Spirit says to the churches.

As you can see, there is an eternal strategy for the love and care of your soul that supersedes any sales deal you may or may not cut today.

If Jesus is your Savior, and you belong to Him, how would you answer the following questions?

Do I talk with Jesus every day and ask Him, as my Advocate in heaven, to help me with my sales disciplines?

Do I also realize that, since I belong to Him, He will speak to God on my behalf on any and every issue?

Just for a moment today, consider your position in the universe as a Christian who sells for a living. We only occupy a tiny place in the midst of a glorious cosmos. Often we get the most upset when we have been lied to, falsely accused, and wronged. We become discouraged when we think we are more important than we really are, and we try to pump ourselves back up by chasing the wrong goals. We become undisciplined.

When we make a mistake, we are able to share that with the living God of the universe, and He *hears our prayers.* That's where our new energy can be found.

When we sin we are commanded by the High Commander to repent. Then Jesus stands up for us *every time* we fail.

Jesus says to God, "Father, that person is one of Mine. He's in My squad. Because of My sacrifice, this soldier is covered by My love!"

And when God looks at you, He doesn't condemn you— He doesn't see what you just did—He sees the blood of Jesus that washes you clean as snow. He sees Jesus' righteousness. Wow, what love! What a perfect Leader!

This incredible canopy of covering in the jungle is called *grace*. We are saved by grace through faith in Christ Jesus. God has built something interesting into grace. While some people might think to take advantage of their right standing with God through Jesus, the person who is truly in His will, will not cheapen that love or take advantage of it in a constant cycle of willful sin and repentance. The man or woman whose heart really belongs to Jesus *wants* to change his or her behavior. And does so.

Sales pro, if there are things that keep making you stumble in the jungle and are stifling your advancement, let today be the day you turn from those things for good. Next time you are tempted to do something against God's will, remember that you're under grace and can choose righteousness *because you want to*. It isn't a matter of guilt or necessity; it's a free choice. You get to choose righteousness!

When you do fall—repent. And remember that Jesus stands up for you as your Advocate with the Father. Jesus will always stand in the gap for you when you are a believer.

Think of His shining face when you make choices in line with God's heart.

Your discipline opens the door to your deliverance by God.

Day Twelve: My Thoughts

Jesus said, "Those whom I love I rebuke and discipline." Why does he do that?

_____

_____

_____

_____

_____

Name a few disciplined leaders who you admire and what makes them successful:

_____

_____

_____

_____

_____

Day Twelve Prayer Requests

--- DAY THIRTEEN ---

Be Still

BASIC FIELD MANUAL

■ *h.* Do not attempt to travel alone at night. Stop early enough in the afternoon to make camp, build a fire, and collect plenty of dead wood before nightfall.

Day Thirteen Verses

God is our refuge and strength, an ever-present help in trouble. Therefore we will not fear, though the earth give way and the mountains fall into the heart of the sea, though its waters roar and foam and the mountains quake with their surging . . .

The LORD Almighty is with us; the God of Jacob is our fortress. Selah. Come and see the works of the LORD, the desolations he has brought on the earth. He makes wars cease to the ends of the earth; he breaks the bow and shatters the spear, he burns the shields with fire. "Be still, and know that I am God; I will be exalted among the nations, I will be exalted in the earth." The LORD Almighty is with us; the God of Jacob is our fortress.

Psalm 46:1-3, 7-11

Day Thirteen Battle Plan

The Lord says, "Be still." It's not the easiest task in the world for salespeople, is it? Yet God has commanded it of us—"Be still." I promise you that one of the most important things that God wants from busy people like us is for us to be still and seek Him.

In fact, I believe He is encouraging us to have a plan that will allow us to be still with Him. Just as it is indicated in the quote from Granddad's manual on the previous page, we have to be prepared to build a camp when we are alone that will provide the best possible chance of survival for us.

One of the most important things a soldier can learn to do in the jungle is to be still and to wait for orders. Any false movement can bring down an attack on top of the soldier, and the same can happen to us if we are not disciplined.

So we must learn to *practice* stillness. It is part of the process of meditating on His Word, getting it inside us, and conditioning our souls to remain strong even in stillness.

Try this: Read the psalm again, and pick some phrases that

stand out. Then, after putting down the book, close your eyes, relax your breathing, and repeat the passages of the psalm that meant something to you.

Be still in God, thinking on His Word. See how long you can do it—rest in the Lord, with His Word on your thoughts. Try it now.

Afterward, check all that apply to how you feel:

___ relaxed

___ capable

___ energized

___ aware

___ thankful

___ peaceful

___ focused

___ balanced

___ blessed

___ other

God calls us to be still so we can break the cycle of doing every-thing ourselves and becoming too busy and works-driven. When we are still, we are more easily drawn into God's presence, and we can more easily listen for God's voice and direction. When we're constantly moving and making noise, we simply can't hear Him very well.

Consider being still before God several times a day. Then

while you are still and have quit making noise—even asking Him for things—pause to see what He might have to say to you.

After you've been truly still with God for a time, pray—converse with Him with all the peace, understanding, and blessing that His Holy Spirit puts inside you. I guarantee it will be a more meaningful conversation with Him than you have ever had before!

When you know that God is alive within you, you will be more inclined to seek out a time for stillness so He can speak to you. More important, you are going for what the Greeks called *enteuxis*: a meeting with God with the intention of having a conversation and asking Him for intercession.

You won't have an easy time being still without practice—it's too easy to let your mind wander onto your tasks for the day, your worries, or your petitions. But with practice, your times with the Lord can lead to listening as well as prayer—a reaching out (*enteuxis*) toward God.

Imagine that! The great I AM wants to be with you, wants to *converse* with you! Begin snatching times of stillness with God today, but practice them from this day forward—rest in His presence.

Don't seek answers, don't ask for anything, and don't *try*. Just *be*—be still.

Day Thirteen Prayer

Dear God,

Help me to be still—it is so hard in today's fast-paced world of deadlines and drive-throughs. I find it hard to focus on You, to rein in my thoughts and really just be still and know that You are God.

Sometimes, God, I confess I get busy, manipulative, and controlling. I try to make our times power sessions of prayer. I do these things because I am afraid of failing. Sometimes I worry too much, and other times I procrastinate or leave out things in my life that really matter.

And even when I am finally still, I am still overwhelmed by You. You are I AM. I'm so thankful for Your love and guidance. Oh, God, help me to pursue being still in You. Remind me during the day that You are the great I AM, and remind me to rest in You.

Thank You. I love You, God.
In Jesus' name I pray. Amen.

Day Thirteen: My Thoughts

List some things that distract you from being still:

_____

_____

_____

_____

_____

_____

List something about God that occurs to you when you are still:

_____

_____

_____

_____

_____

_____

Day Thirteen Prayer Requests

The Importance of Salt

BASIC FIELD MANUAL

■ 16. USE OF SALT.—Sweat results in the loss of fluid and salt (sodium chloride) from the body. Under ordinary conditions sufficient salt and fluid are eaten and drunk to replace the loss, but during heavy muscular exercise the loss of fluid and salt through perspiration may be excessive. Thirst is created, and further intake of water alone merely results in additional loss of salt. The symptoms of heat cramp may develop.

Day Fourteen Verses

You are the salt of the earth. But if the salt loses its saltiness, how can it be made salty again? It is no longer good for anything, except to be thrown out and trampled by men.

Matthew 5:13

Be joyful always; pray continually; give thanks in all circumstances, for this is God's will for you in Christ Jesus.

1 Thessalonians 5:16-18

For you created my inmost being; you knit me together in my mother's womb. I praise you because I am fearfully and wonderfully made; your works are wonderful, I know that full well.

Psalm 139:13-14

Day Fourteen Battle Plan

The use of salt has always been critical to the survival of people, and people who are often placed under physical stress, like soldiers and athletes and manual laborers, have to be extra careful to maintain proper levels of salt in their bodies. Too low, and what was just a difficult march or workout can turn into a life-threatening event.

We recognize that our difficulties sometimes come from our own inability to remember who we are in the eyes of God. We are "a royal priesthood" as we are reminded by Peter.

In the sales jungle, we must remember our training and our calling despite the tough times and difficult circumstances. We must retain our saltiness and ensure that we are not thrown out and trampled by those who have a different agenda.

The first step is to remember that God is with you. You must sprinkle a little salt on your battle wounds and give thanks *anyway*, even in the middle of your rough spots.

God created you with your specific talents and gifts. He knows exactly who you are and who you are becoming, because He made you. If you are a natural salesperson, it is because God made you the way you are—He gave you an ability to persuade others, made you innately likable, gave you infectious joy and enthusiasm, and has made you able to handle the pressure of your deadlines and expectations. He built you to order. God is the Master Planner and has wonderful ideas for your life.

Today meditate on a few of your best character traits. Then pull two or three of them out of your spiritual quiver and use them to take aim on your sales targets. Take those gifts and talents that God gave you and fulfill your God-given destiny! And while you are out there setting the world on fire, praise Him!

Sing with gusto in your car, pray with fervor on the train, shout out loud in the parking lot, or jump for joy in the airport—praise Him!

Make people wonder about you and why you are so salty for God! They should have the chance to see someone being rewarded for following God's plan with the joy that wells up within. Let that joy spill out onto others.

Have you joyfully thanked God today for
making you the way He did? Stop right now
and think of three things that you're
thankful for about yourself. Then thank
Him for three things you see Him working
on, especially if those things have
become more clear to you while you have
been reading this field manual:

_____

_____

_____

_____

_____

_____

Learn to become aware when things start to steal your joy
and remove your effectiveness for God.

Today we see the world changing rapidly. Layoffs frighten
and impact our friends and family. Television and radio news
programs exclaim the torture and the terror that have come
to characterize the times we live in. We find our conversations
sprinkled with patriotic passion as the world rushes toward
chaos. Even our own children are so much more savvy and
worldly at earlier ages.

We sometimes take those multiple pressures and throw them
into a bubbling pot of high-pressure performance requirements,

and we come to God beat up and ready to collapse. We stumble out of the sales jungle with a glazed look in our eyes, and we are sometimes unrecognizable to our own families.

God loves it when we come to Him like that because we are trusting His promise to restore our joy so that we can go back out as "the salt of the earth."

Consider this promise from God: "The LORD will keep you from all harm—he will watch over your life; the LORD will watch over your coming and going both now and forevermore" (Psalm 121:7–8).

You are fearfully and wonderfully made—go and do what you were born to do. And while you're at it, praise God and look for chances to share your joy!

Day Fourteen Prayer

Dear God,

Thank You for making me just the way I am. I know You created me with a purpose in mind and gave me all the attributes, skills, and potential I need to be successful—and You created me with a plan. Thank You for shaping me in my mother's womb.

Lord, You are always faithful to me—You teach me, refine me, and guide me. You give me opportunities each day to show others the joy You put inside me, and I pray that I will see these chances and act on them. Help me to represent

You to everyone I come in contact with—my family, customers, and even total strangers.

Teach me to pray as I see news stories that begin to steal my joy.

God, help me to only use the talents and gifts You gave me to Your glory. Let me provide for my family and be a blessing to my employer.

Let a song of worship rise up in my heart, one that lifts You up!

Thank You, Lord, for hearing my joyful sound.

In Jesus' name I pray. Amen.

Day Fourteen: My Thoughts

List three national or world events that have captured your attention but have impacted your joy. Pray over those right now and consider that God is sovereign.

_____

_____

_____

_____

_____

_____

Thank God for giving you the ability to be the salt of the earth. What is He asking from you for your work today?

_____

_____

_____

_____

_____

_____

Day Fourteen Prayer Requests

_____

_____

_____

_____

_____

_____

A Worthy Battalion

BASIC FIELD MANUAL

Staff Data For Jungle Warfare

	Number of Men (1 squad)	Distance (yards)	Width (yards)	Area (square yards)	Hours	Tools
Trail breaking	12	3,000	2/3	2,000	3–6	Machetes
Trail clearing	12	1,000	1	1,000	12	Machetes, axes
Bridge building (animal)	12	6	3	18	4	Do.
Corduroying, cutting and placing	12	100	3	300	12	Do.
Area clearing	12	1,000	1	1,000	12	Do.
Trail blocking	12	Time for felling trees				Do.e
Road building, dirt, passable for 1 vehicle	12	50	3	150	12	Machetes, axes, shovels, picks
Fire lane cutting	12	1,000	2	2,000	18	Machetes, axes
Tree felling (cutting)	2	Can fell a single tree from 10 to 20 inches in diameter in 15–45 minutes				Axes

Day Fifteen Verses

Therefore, since we are surrounded by such a great cloud of witnesses, let us throw off everything that hinders and the sin that so easily entangles, and let us run with perseverance the race marked out for us. Let us fix our eyes on Jesus, the author and perfecter of our faith, who for the joy set before him endured the cross, scorning its shame, and sat down at the right hand of the throne of God. Consider him who endured such opposition from sinful men, so that you will not grow weary and lose heart.

Hebrews 12:1-3

Do not be anxious about anything, but in everything, by prayer and petition, with thanksgiving, present your requests to God. And the peace of God, which transcends all understanding, will guard your hearts and your minds in Christ Jesus.

Philippians 4:6-7

Day Fifteen Battle Plan

In the NFL, teams always hope for home-field advantage when they have to face their toughest opponents. There's nothing quite like the cheers of the crowd to move you toward victory.

I am always moved, however, when I attend an NFL game,

and the loudest cheers come from the fans when they recognize the men and women of our Armed Services. They stand, they take off their hats, they cheer wildly, they whistle, and some even shed a tear . . . including me. The sacrifice is so evident. It makes me proud to stand for our military members when they are willing to die for our freedoms.

As a salesperson, you may not feel you have too many people cheering for you, yet the Hebrews writer tells you that you are *surrounded* by a great cloud of witnesses! Your life is lived out to the cheering of the saints who have gone to heaven ahead of you, and they root you on, much in the same way we cheer for our athletes—look at the Hebrews passage again and notice the sports language.

We are in a race! But we are not on our own. We have fans.

Yet, if you focus only on your mundane, earthly details, you will miss the point. The saints in this crowd above cheer for us as we pursue our real prize—the author and perfecter of our faith, Jesus. *Fix your eyes on Him first*; then ask Him to join you as you focus on your new products, daily sales objectives, or quotas for the year!

You can see from the Jungle Warfare chart (p. 107) that a successful squad is built of specialists and trained people who each understand their individual duty and responsibility. Once again, it's obvious that preplanning is the key to survival in the sales jungle—and that you should not go after your objectives *alone.*

Great soldiers succeed and persevere through adversity not because practice makes perfect, but because they perfect their practice habits—they do things habitually in training that will make them habitually successful during the battle. Great salespeople do the same thing.

Let me tell you about the single greatest habit you can have as a salesperson: *Pray Before You Sell.* If you are an acronym person, remember—PBYS. Let this become your mantra. Here is an example of how you might pray:

- Ask God to make your words honest and full of integrity.
- Ask God to prepare your customers' ears and hearts to receive your message.
- Ask God to remind you of His love while you are selling.
- Ask God to help you close the sale.
- Thank Him.

When you are selling, thank God for being with you. Then run the race set before you, imagining the crowd of saints who cheer you on as you press toward the goal. When I am selling, I often think of my two grandfathers, who are both in heaven, and how proud they must be that I am working with Christ in my heart—just as they used to work.

Day Fifteen Prayer

Dear God,

Today I ask You to prepare my thoughts and words so that they are orderly and full of integrity. Condition my mind to think rapidly and with great insight so that I might respond wisely to my customers' inquiries. Prepare them to buy from me so that my products and services might be pleasing to them.

Thank You in advance, Lord, that You are already moving on my behalf. Help me to make a habit of praying before I sell.

Thank You that I am not in this human race alone—that You are always with me, and that the saints who have gone before me cheer me on. Help me to run the sales race with perseverance and to be anxious for nothing but pray about everything. In Jesus' name I pray. Amen.

Day Fifteen: My Thoughts

Name your top customers below, and ask God what needs they may have:

_____

_____

_____

_____

_____

_____

Think about someone in your life who is
your greatest champion. If that person is
still alive, get in touch with him or her
this week and recharge your batteries. If
the individual is not alive, thank God
for his or her influence in your life,
and write down four or five sentences
this person would say to you if he or she
were with you right now:

_____

_____

_____

_____

_____

Day Fifteen Prayer Requests

_____

_____

_____

_____

_____

--- DAY SIXTEEN ---

Lift Up from Below

BASIC FIELD MANUAL

■ d. Next to his machete, a good pocket knife is a man's most useful possession in the jungle.

Day Sixteen Verses

You give me your shield of victory, and your right hand sustains me; you stoop down to make me great.

Psalms 18:35

While he [*Jesus*] was in Bethany, reclining at the table in the home of a man known as Simon the Leper, a woman came with an alabaster jar of very expensive perfume, made of pure nard. She broke the jar and poured the perfume on his head. Some of those present were saying indignantly to one another, "Why this waste of perfume? It could have been sold for more than a year's wages and the money given to the poor." And they rebuked her harshly. "Leave her alone," said Jesus. "Why are you bothering her? She has done a beautiful thing to me."

Mark 14:3-6

Day Sixteen Battle Plan

Today I chose the excerpt from Granddad's field manual because it mentions the importance of a pocketknife as man's "most useful possession." Every day, I carry a pocketknife with the name "Granddad Sykes" stamped on it. His pocketknife is a constant reminder of how he carried himself as a man and how he always had time for me. Always.

He used to call me "Old Buddy," and he knew the great value of how to spend time with me. I know that I really was his buddy—his friend—and that he loved me.

God (and many granddads) are prone to bending down and sharing great wisdom. From them we learn the importance of giving of ourselves.

Today's first verse, from Psalms, gives us a perfect example of how God reaches us—He bends low to lift us up. What an image! And can you imagine the overwhelming love that woman in Mark 14 must have had for Christ? She knelt at His feet, took the vial of perfume from around her neck— where she carried it close to her heart—and then poured out a *year's wages*! (How much did you make last year? Could you pour that out as an expression of your love for Jesus? Think about that for a minute, and then move on to the rest of today's lesson.)

Jesus knelt at His disciples' feet and washed them, showing true servanthood and illustrating that we lead others by serving them. God calls us to be servants to those around us—we are to stoop down to make others great.

My parents and my grandparents have always been such great inspirational teachers for me. They have always sacrificed so that I might have more, and they have always given of themselves. Who has been an inspirational teacher for you? Do you carry anything with you that helps remind you of how they were willing to give of their time to teach you about life?

I believe we all are called to carry "spiritual pocketknives" that represent the lessons and experiences we've received from others and that are to be counted among our most important possessions for use in our march through the jungle.

The woman in today's Scripture carried around a vial of perfume. It was precious to her, yet, in the presence of Christ, she was able to share it freely.

How long has it been since you served someone else? I'm not talking about opening the door for someone or saying a kind word. When was the last time you literally gave up something that was *very valuable* and offered it to someone else?

For a moment, think about whether you are only serving

yourself (like any salesperson can do) or whether you have a higher calling.

I have a competitor who has been in my line of work for much longer than I have, yet I have the majority of the business from our shared customer. Not long ago, in the middle of a negotiation, my competitor realized that although his knowledge was far superior to mine on the topic, he also realized that my product was better for the customer in a very specific application. His wisdom superseded his ambition, and he showed me (and the customer) why he has been successful for many years: he recommended *my product instead of his* for the customer's specific need and instantly became more valuable in the eyes of the customer. Yep, *you can tell the truth* and be in sales!

Servant-selling asks us to tell the truth regardless of the immediacy of the moment. It asks us to consider reaching into our hearts and recalling the lessons we have learned from our greatest teachers, and then it asks for more—it asks us to consider giving "our most useful possession." What is your most useful possession?

By practicing servant-selling, we tap into an eternal ability to share wisdom and insight based on non-negotiable virtues—rather than merely exercising temporal sales skills that soon bite us in the cargo shorts and tarnish our reputations.

I hope you have been practicing being still; these are the times you will hear God—because you are listening. As you do this, as you grow in your faith, the Holy Spirit will put into your mind the thought of someone you need to serve. It will not always be easy to hear God's voice and understand His direction while you are busy working and selling. This is why we must practice being still and listening—and then serving others.

The Bible tells us that sometimes when we serve strangers, we are actually ministering to angels without being aware of it (see Hebrews 13:2). Whom will you serve today? A competitor? A customer? A colleague? A manager? Another sales rep? A neighbor? A child? An angel? Today you are called to see Christ in that person and to pour yourself into him or her by *being Christ* to that individual.

> Stop right now, pause, and be still before the Lord. Ask Him whom He might want you to serve today. Be still and listen. If God puts a specific person on your heart, write his or her name down:
>
> "Today, I am going to go see (or call) _____ and I will serve him/her today by _____."

If God does not give you a special person, keep your eyes open during your day—He *will* bring someone across your path. Stoop down to make that person great by serving as Jesus did. You will be a blessing to that person, and you will make the jungle life more bearable for someone else.

Day Sixteen Prayer

Thank You for the merciful service of Your Son, Jesus Christ. In Him, we have the perfect example of selfless love. Thank You also, Lord, for those teachers who have given so much to get us where we are today. Bless them and encourage them as they serve without any need for recognition but just out of a sense of love.

Now, Lord, show me the person You want me to serve today. Help him or her to be receptive to my help. Help me to be honest and courageous enough to follow through on my promise. Help me to seek You and to really give something of value.

Holy Spirit, I will need Your protection today: please go before me, remain with me, and follow hard behind me. In Jesus' name I pray. Amen.

Day Sixteen: My Thoughts

What are some everyday things you can do to bless and serve people?

Are there specific people you should
especially serve? Write their names here.
(Don't forget your family!)

_____

_____

_____

_____

_____

Day Sixteen Prayer Requests

_____

_____

_____

_____

_____

--- DAY SEVENTEEN ---

Semper Fidelis

Day Seventeen Verses

Not to us, O LORD, not to us but to your name be the glory, because of your love and faithfulness.

Psalm 115:1

I love the LORD, for he heard my voice; he heard my cry for mercy. Because he turned his ear to me, I will call on him as long as I live.

Psalm 116:1-2

Praise the LORD, all you nations; extol him, all you peoples. For great is his love toward us, and the faithfulness of the LORD endures forever. Praise the LORD.

Psalm 117:1-2

Day Seventeen Battle Plan

Semper fidelis is a Latin phrase meaning "always faithful." It is the motto of the U.S. Marine Corps and has been used over the centuries to denote a devotion to cause above personal gain. As salespeople, we often put personal gain over cause. Inherently, this kind of thinking taps into a selfish mind-set . . . coaching us to believe that we are entitled to our unfair share.

What I am about to reveal to you is counter to every other sales book you have read or will read: be *always faithful* to God. Know Him like the Marine knows his rifle; know Him like Jesus knew Him; know Him so that you can fight the sales fight with poise, performance, and persistence.

I recently read a story about four U.S. Marines who reunited after they had enlisted together—fifty years ago. They served together in the Radar Squadron, Third Marine Air Wing, until October 1961, and they rejoined each other to keep their bond of *Semper Fidelis* strong. They were obedient to their original commitment.

For two weeks now, you have been obedient to engaging the God of the universe. You have confessed your sins, discovered

God's Son anew, trusted God for business insights—and received His blessings as well as His commandments.

God loves you and is aware of your faithful commitment.

During this last week, you will stretch your thinking and grow in your spiritual understanding. This can be like a spiritual boot camp, if you push yourself to find out more about how far your faithfulness to God can take you.

Take a few moments right now to look back at what God has been doing in your life in the jungle over these two weeks.

Has God blessed a customer in a special way through you?

Have you learned something new about your relationship with God through meditating on His Word or in prayer?

If so, take a few moments to thank Him for being faithful, and then write it down.

By seeing these two weeks through, you have shown you are committed to knowing Him better. Your obedience and faithfulness to God will continue to produce abundance for you—but most important, it is already producing a deeper relationship with God.

Ask God how He wants you to be faithful to Him today. Take just a moment this morning (or whenever you are reading this) and ask God what He might have you do today—ask Him what you can do to especially please Him *today*.

Have you been practicing being still? If not, you might turn back to Day Thirteen and follow the steps again. Be still before the Lord, and ask to hear His voice—and really expect to hear from Him! Pause long enough to hear from your Father.

And whatever He says, do it. *Semper Fi.*

Day Seventeen Prayer

O Lord, how majestic is Your name in all the earth! Great is Thy faithfulness. Better is one day in Your courts than a thousand elsewhere!

Dear God, I am living a new reality, understanding just a little bit more each day about how incredible You are. As the psalms I read today testify, Your faithfulness endures forever!

For the next five days, I am praying for spiritual insight: let me better see the world through Your eyes, and empower me to be a person after Your own heart. Dear Lord, put me in places where I can serve You. Here am I, Lord; send me.

I love You, God.
I love You, Jesus.
I love You, Holy Spirit. Amen.

Day Seventeen: My Thoughts

Write down what God has shown you in these two weeks that helps you understand that He is always faithful.

_____
_____
_____
_____
_____
_____

We are all called to be *always faithful* to God. In your sales career, where is God urging you to be more faithful to Him as your Commander and Chief?

_____
_____
_____
_____
_____
_____

Day Seventeen Prayer Requests

Army Ants

BASIC FIELD MANUAL

■ 5. ANTS (FORMIDICAE).—a. *General.*—Ants are so well known that a description of these insects is unnecessary. There are a few kinds that bite, a few that sting, and a few that both bite and sting. The biting ants are carnivorous (flesh eating), and the larger varieties have been known to attack men weakened by disease or wounded. They rapidly overwhelm the victim by the great numbers which attack simultaneously. The sting-ing ants inflict painful injuries by the injection of formic acid. The sting of some species is so pain-ful that natives roll in agony on the ground.

Day Eighteen Verses

In the name of the Lord Jesus Christ, we command you, brothers, to keep away from every brother who is idle and does not live according to the teaching you received from us. For you yourselves know how you ought to follow our example. We were not idle when we were with you, nor did we eat anyone's food without paying for it. On the contrary, we worked night and day, laboring and toiling so that we would not be a burden to any of you. We did this, not because we do not have the right to such help, but in order to make ourselves a model for you to follow. For even when we were with you, we gave you this rule: "If a man will not work, he shall not eat."

2 Thessalonians 3:6-10

Day Eighteen Battle Plan

Take a look at Proverbs 6:6–11:

> *Go to the ant, you sluggard;*
> *consider its ways and be wise!*
> *It has no commander,*
> *no overseer or ruler,*
> *yet it stores its provisions in summer*

and gathers its food at harvest.
How long will you lie there, you sluggard?
When will you get up from your sleep?
A little sleep, a little slumber,
a little folding of the hands to rest—
and poverty will come on you like a bandit
and scarcity like an armed man.

Have you ever considered these verses from the Bible before? As a Christian salesperson, what do they stir up inside of you? Have you taken the concept of working without ceasing *too* seriously? Have you ever blurred the line between being diligent and finding your identity and self-worth from your accomplishments?

My friend, if you are a workaholic . . . heed my warning and take these verses with a grain of salt and not as a biblical excuse to feed your need for performance-based recognition.

I'll say it again—be *careful with these verses and with a workaholic spirit.* Many men and women have worked themselves right out of marriages.

Why even include these verses as part of our devotions in this book, you might wonder, when they sound so much like what we hear every day from our managers, inner voices, loved ones, and especially the world? These words seem to press us to work harder, rather than trusting in God to provide, don't they?

No. They are a reminder that we were put here on earth by God to work.

"So God created man in his own image, in the image of God he created him; male and female he created them. God blessed them and said to them, "Be fruitful and increase in number; fill the earth and subdue it. Rule over the fish of the sea and the birds of the air and over every living creature that moves on the ground" (Genesis 1:27–28).

In fact, I'm the first to agree that sometimes, some of us *do* need a little kick in the rear, a jump-start, or something to help us get reenergized—motivated. Many people need to be reminded of these verses about the ant—they need a push toward diligence.

I do not think I am exaggerating, however, to say that any salesperson who needs these reminders constantly will not last in our profession. In today's economic climate, there might be a thousand people who want your job right now; you must stay motivated to keep it. As a Christian in sales, you must go a step further and ask yourself: *What really motivates me to be successful?*

I included these verses because we need to remember something very important as we deal with questions about our self-worth. You must ask yourself, *Do I gain my sense of self-worth from my accomplishments, or do I gain it through my relationship with God?*

God has given you incredible gifts, but sometimes using them can be exhausting. And when we are exhausted, we often try harder to control our lives instead of seeking God's will. Remember, you are seeking a new balance: learning to rest in the Lord and then, after resting in God, being obedient to His plan for your life. I also understand that while it would be wonderful to rest in the Lord forever, we must all come down from the mountaintop and reengage with the practical demands of this world.

I get after my sales numbers every day, and so must you.

I provide for my family every day—and so must you.

Understand that God isn't interested in having you live the rest of your life in silent contemplation. He has a plan for you, and it includes things only *you* can do.

But we all have to make sure that we are not working ourselves to death. Remember the disciples' question: "Lord, to whom shall we go? You have the words of eternal life." Those wonderful words of life are where we must begin if we are going to understand how to balance our work, our family, and our lives. Do you know the great hymn "Wonderful Words of Life"? "Words of life and beauty, teach me faith and duty; beautiful words, wonderful words, wonderful words of life . . ."

Seek God first and His wonderful words of life. Be still in Him. But when that time is over, it's time to go to work with renewed vigor. You must engage in the sales jungle *for Him!*

Day Eighteen Prayer

Dear God,

Some days are harder than others—sometimes I feel the weight of providing for my family very keenly, and it is easy for me to focus on my work as my source of worth.

But You have called me to praise You regardless of my circumstances—easy or hard. I know in You I can be satisfied with much or little. Thank You that You never change and are everlasting—thank You for always being faithful! Your steadfast love is awe inspiring.

Lord, thank You for Your ready strength and encouragement. Let me feel them today as I see the rising and setting of the sun, tireless in the arc in which You put it. You put Adam in the garden to work it, so I know You intended me to work. Thank You for equipping me.

Father God, today let me go to work like Your ant: full of boldness and with the confidence that You will give me the strength I will need to accomplish any heavy tasks. Let me remember that Your Son, Jesus Christ, was able to carry the sins of the world on His shoulders and that I can find my strength in Him today even as He found His strength in You. I love You, God. Amen.

Day Eighteen: My Thoughts

Sometimes I feel as though my identity
and my job are tied together because:

_____

_____

_____

_____

_____

I know my worth goes beyond my ability to
provide because:

_____

_____

_____

_____

_____

Day Eighteen Prayer Requests

Pray for Your Enemy

BASIC FIELD MANUAL

■ 70. CONTACT WITH ENEMY.—*a. Conduct of leading elements.*—(1) Easily controlled formations should be maintained as long as the situation permits—ordinarily until first contact with the enemy. When hostile elements are encountered, scouts and patrols move against and endeavor to overcome the advance enemy detachments rapidly and with the least possible noise or disturbance.

Day Nineteen Verses

Do not repay anyone evil for evil. Be careful to do what is right in the eyes of everybody. If it is possible, as far as it depends on you, live at peace with everyone. Do not take revenge, my friends, but leave room for God's wrath, for it is written: "It is mine to avenge; I will repay," says the Lord. On the contrary: "If your enemy is hungry, feed him; if he is thirsty, give him something to drink. In doing this, you will heap burning coals on his head." Do not be overcome by evil, but overcome evil with good.

Romans 12:17-21

"You have heard that it was said, 'Love your neighbor and hate your enemy.' But I tell you: Love your enemies and pray for those who persecute you, that you may be sons of your Father in heaven. He causes his sun to rise on the evil and the good, and sends rain on the righteous and the unrighteous."

Matthew 5:43-45

Day Nineteen Battle Plan

Brace yourself, sales soldier. Your task for today is *to pray for your enemies—yes, even your competitors*. Ouch! But what do I pray for those no-good, rotten scoundrels? Well, why not pray that your competitor will receive Jesus Christ as Lord? That'll fix him!

In the movie *Fiddler on the Roof*, one of the characters asks his rabbi, "Is there a proper blessing for the Tzar?" The wise old rabbi thinks for a minute and says, "A blessing for the Tzar? Of course. May God bless and keep the Tzar . . . far away from us!"

That's a great prayer for our enemies, and one I have prayed many times. But how much greater would it be if each of your competitors were to have a personal relationship with God Almighty—a relationship that changed his or her behavior? Then you would know that the Holy Spirit would be working on him day and night (just as the Holy Spirit works on you) to encourage him to work as though he were working for the Lord. Remember, their eternal destination may hang in the balance.

In Luke, Jesus tells us we might be working side by side with someone when He comes again (Luke 17:28–35). In some cases, one will be taken and the other left. Jesus said, "On that day no one who is on the roof of his house, with his goods inside, should go down to get them" (v. 31). You can't take it with you, and neither can your competitors.

That verse helps put into perspective what is important to God, doesn't it? It begins to give you an eternal picture of God's power and purpose for your life. Hopefully, it encourages you to pray for your loved ones, competitors, and even your enemies—and to forgive them. In fact, if someone sins against you seven times in a day, Jesus said that as long as that person comes back seven times and *earnestly repents*, then you are called to *forgiveness* (Luke 17:3–4).

Now, I'm not talking about constantly running a fool's errand. You know when enough is enough. Win your sales battles, but leave the repayment of any wrongs done to you in the Lord's hands.

In Matthew 10:11–13, Jesus says:

"Whatever town or village you enter, search for some worthy person there and stay at his house until you leave. As you enter the home, give it your greeting. If the home is deserving, let your peace rest on it; if it is not, let your peace return to you."

Jesus was talking to the disciples about their impending journey for the gospel. What do you notice about Christ's instruction to them regarding people who would not receive them? How might this pertain to your witnessing efforts?

Verse 16 of that same chapter is especially interesting: "I am sending you out like sheep among wolves. Therefore, be as shrewd as snakes and as innocent as doves."

As you go out into the jungle, you are called to be both caring and shrewd. In our line of work, those are two great attributes to carry in a sales bag.

Day Nineteen: My Prayer

Dear God, You are an awesome and powerful God. And I come to You for help today.

Sometimes, I get so caught up in my material life. It is easy to get angry with anyone who stands in my way, but You are such a loving and forgiving God, and through Your

Son, Jesus Christ, You have called me to be loving and forgiving too. Help me to pray for my competitors as well as my friends. I pray that they will receive Christ—even the ones I count as my enemies!

Dear God, please keep my enemies far away from me. But . . . if You should choose for me to share my faith with them, let me push my pride aside and find the courage to be obedient to Your direction. Help me to be as wise as a serpent and as gentle as a dove.

And finally, when it comes to dealing with my competition and my enemies, let me always seek You first. In Jesus' name I pray. Amen.

Day Nineteen: My Thoughts

List some people you count as enemies. Ask God for their salvation and any specific needs they may have that God can answer to open a door for you to minister to them.

It is hard when my competition does the
following:

_____

_____

_____

_____

_____

_____

List a few things God might have you do
to respond to this:

_____

_____

_____

_____

_____

_____

Day Nineteen Prayer Requests

_____

_____

_____

_____

_____

_____

Advance

BASIC FIELD MANUAL

■ 69. ADVANCE.—a. *Formation.*—(1) The formation for the advance must be carefully organized to assure the maximum of control and the maintenance of direction. (An important objective in training for combat in jungle areas must be thorough familiarity by all individuals with the means and methods of determining and maintaining direction.)

Day Twenty Verses

In the same way, the Spirit helps us in our weakness. We do not know what we ought to pray for, but the Spirit himself intercedes for us with groans that words cannot express. And he who searches our hearts knows the mind of the Spirit, because the Spirit intercedes for the saints in accordance with God's will. And we know that in all things God works for the good of those who love him, who have been called according to his purpose.

Romans 8:26-28

Day Twenty Battle Plan

I have always identified very strongly with Peter. He was deeply in love with Jesus and exclaimed Him to be the Son of God, yet he also took matters into his own hands over and over again instead of trusting Jesus, much as I have in my personal and professional life.

Do you recall the story of Jesus walking on the water one night? At first, as they were sitting in the boat, the disciples thought they were seeing a ghost! As boldly as any great salesperson who summons the courage to get out of his comfort zone and to make something happen, it was Peter who said, "Lord, if it is you, tell me to come to you." Peter stepped out onto the water with the waves; it must have been hard for him to do.

Those of us who sell for a living realize that if we want to be successful at our jobs, we have to step into opportunities with great resolve and a strong sense of confidence. Some days, when we are riding high, stepping out is easy. On other days, when the storm is brewing around us, it is harder, isn't it?

How many times have you stepped out of the boat, wanting

to follow Christ, only to flounder when you saw wind-whipped waves all around you? What do you say to God when times are tough—when sales are bad, your boss is on your case, or when you are desperate for peace? How do you pray?

The Bible says that the Holy Spirit can help you pray and that He will even pray *for you* when you don't know what to say!

Today, practice moving from sitting in the boat to feeling God's Spirit within the depths of your soul. Being able to feel God in this way will give you the capacity to draw upon a very deep spiritual truth, and it will provide comfort for you when you are in the storms of life and in need. (You'll need to be somewhere where you won't be interrupted and can take a few moments.)

Close your eyes, take a deep breath, relax, and breathe easy. Now, think about being in the boat on the lake. Watch Jesus come toward you. See Him standing on the water and reaching out His hands to you.

Now open your mouth to speak to Jesus—what do you say to Him? Will your words be enough? Try to express everything you're feeling to Him. As you feel the depth of your love for Jesus and your reliance on the Holy Spirit, now step out of the boat . . . let Jesus embrace you.

What are you feeling right now?

Speak the words out loud. Those beautiful, precious sounds you are making to Jesus is the Spirit groaning and praying for you. They are both natural and supernatural.

They have been there inside of you since you received God's Spirit, and you should pray this way to help you when you are afraid, in despair, or when you just can't find the right words to pray to God.

Now continue to pray quietly in the Spirit, locked in communion with God. Enjoy God's sweet presence. Know that you can come here anytime and stay as long as you like. In fact, you can also practice finding this presence and staying in it during the course of your sales day. No weapon formed against you will prosper. This weapon of Spirit-led prayer is the ultimate tool for life in the jungle.

As you come near the end of your study of Jungle Warfare, I want to make sure that I have challenged you to grow as a Christian. The tools and resources you have to defeat the enemy, to advance God's kingdom, and to find your own place in His kingdom are powerful, and when you know how to use them you will not be defeated.

Day Twenty Prayer

Dear God,

I have been given a gift. Knowing that Your Holy Spirit is alive within me and is there to teach me, console me, and pray to You for me is amazing. You are my Creator, my Redeemer, the One who calls me onto the waves, and my Abba Father. When I need to, let me cry out to You so that

You can comfort and heal me even when I lack the words. Let me be caught in Your Holy Spirit, so that I can be in constant communication with You.

I love You. Jesus, thank You for interceding for me. Amen.

Day Twenty: My Thoughts

Write out how you felt about today's meditative exercise, and name three new adventures you believe God is calling you to attempt with His guidance:

_____

_____

_____

_____

_____

What has God shown you in your times of stillness and prayer in the Spirit?

_____

_____

_____

_____

_____

Day Twenty Prayer Requests

On Patrol

BASIC FIELD MANUAL

■ *b.* Initial dispositions should be such that all obstacles, and all trails or other approaches leading into or around the position are covered by security groups to the front and flanks. The commander must assure himself that avenues of approach over which a hostile enveloping force might strike his flanks or rear are adequately guarded. All approaches between the defensive position and the security detachments are patrolled to prevent hostile elements from breaking through the jungle and cutting off these security elements.

Day Twenty-one Verses

Finally, all of you, live in harmony with one another; be sympathetic, love as brothers, be compassionate and humble. Do not repay evil with evil or insult with insult, but with blessing, because to this you were called so that you may inherit a blessing. For, "Whoever would love life and see good days must keep his tongue from evil and his lips from deceitful speech. He must turn from evil and do good; he must seek peace and pursue it. For the eyes of the Lord are on the righteous and his ears are attentive to their prayer, but the face of the Lord is against those who do evil." . . .

Always be prepared to give an answer to everyone who asks you to give the reason for the hope that you have. But do this with gentleness and respect, keeping a clear conscience, so that those who speak maliciously against your good behavior in Christ may be ashamed of their slander. It is better, if it is God's will, to suffer for doing good than for doing evil. For Christ died for sins once for all, the righteous for the unrighteous, to bring you to God.

1 Peter 3:8-12, 15-18

Day Twenty-one Battle Plan

Yesterday, you learned how to unbridle your tongue for the purpose of allowing God's Spirit to pray through you. Take that newfound gift and practice it anytime you want to commune with God.

Today, though, I am asking you to consider *bridling* your tongue. In Proverbs 6:12–15 God's Word says:

> *A scoundrel and villain,*
> *who goes about with a corrupt mouth,*
> *who winks with his eye,*
> *signals with his feet*
> *and motions with his fingers,*
> *who plots evil with deceit in his heart—*
> *he always stirs up dissension.*
> *Therefore disaster will overtake him in an instant;*
> *he will suddenly be destroyed—without remedy.*

Now consider these words from James 3:5–11:

> *Likewise the tongue is a small part of the body, but it makes great boasts. Consider what a great forest is set on fire by a small spark. The tongue also is a fire, a world of evil among the parts of the body. It corrupts the whole*

person, sets the whole course of his life on fire, and is itself set on fire by hell.

All kinds of animals, birds, reptiles and creatures of the sea are being tamed and have been tamed by man, but no man can tame the tongue. It is a restless evil, full of deadly poison.

With the tongue we praise our Lord and Father, and with it we curse men, who have been made in God's likeness. Out of the same mouth come praise and cursing. My brothers, this should not be. Can both fresh water and salt water flow from the same spring?

It is almost a certainty that one of your greatest abilities lies in your silver-tongued persuasiveness. Using your persuasiveness is a natural ability that has served you well, and it will continue to do so for the rest of your life.

However, today practice letting the Holy Spirit bridle your tongue. All day long, *check every word* you say with the Holy Spirit *before* you say it. Ask yourself, *Is what I am about to say true, above reproach, kind, building someone up, and/or full of integrity?* If not, ask the Holy Spirit what you should say.

You may have noticed that the excerpt from Granddad's field manual for today (Day Twenty-one) reminds us to protect against anything that might be considered an obstacle. As a hostile element, the enemy will break through the jungle and attack if you do not patrol and prevent a breach in security. You must perform the same type of reconnaissance on your tongue.

You may have had this experience: a competitor begins to talk about his product with one of your clients, possibly disparaging what you offer. It's tempting to respond in kind. I remember one particular time I fell into that trap; later, my customer gently said, "Chris, don't do that again. You aren't like the other guys, and that kind of stuff brings you down to their level."

You see, even though what I had shared was true, it was not kind and it was not full of integrity. The customer probably could have received my message (which was true) if I had used a better method to share my information. As salespeople, our method and our message must *both* be above reproach. Otherwise, the enemy will use it to attack us from all angles.

Rather than rolling yourself in the mud, let your customers see the light of Christ in you. They will be so attracted to it, they will love you for it, and you will not need to mix any dirt into your methods to justify your products over those of your competitors. Take the high road of integrity, and bridle your tongue.

The things you say today—the jokes you tell, the words you whisper, the e-mails you forward, the positions you take—all have an eternal impact. Choose carefully.

Day Twenty-one Prayer

Dear God, You know how hard it is for me to control my tongue. You have given me my ability to speak, but help me to guard my words more carefully today and from now on. Help me to take a higher road of integrity, even when I'm tempted to descend to the mud and start slinging.

Your Word tells me that my words have the power to move mountains. Let me accept that awesome responsibility in a sober and thoughtful manner. If I stumble, grant me the courage to sincerely apologize and set the record straight.

Make me a person of integrity. Make my word my bond. In Jesus' name I pray. Amen.

Day Twenty-one: My Thoughts

I need God's help with my tongue concerning the following:

List a time when you said something you should not have said, another time when God checked your words, and the outcomes of both:

_____

_____

_____

_____

_____

_____

Day Twenty-one Prayer Requests

_____

_____

_____

_____

_____

_____

--- DAY TWENTY-TWO ---

Run into Battle!

BASIC FIELD MANUAL

■ *b.* Small, determined groups can delay forces many times their size; however, this type of combat in jungle areas is especially tiring. Consequently, units should be divided into groups so that they may alternate in the occupation of delaying positions and thus secure rest, while the enemy is kept constantly engaged.

Day Twenty-two Verses

I thank my God every time I remember you. In all my prayers for all of you, I always pray with joy because of your partnership in the gospel from the first day until now, being confident of this, that he who began a good work in you will carry it on to completion until the day of Christ Jesus.

Philippians 1:3–6

Therefore, my dear brothers, stand firm. Let nothing move you. Always give yourselves fully to the work of the Lord, because you know that your labor in the Lord is not in vain.

1 Corinthians 15:58

Day Twenty-two Battle Plan

Today is graduation day!

You have taken the challenge issued twenty-two days ago, and you are about to fulfill your commitment. Congratulations! May God continue to richly bless you in all of your endeavors.

For your final assignment, consider the life of King David. David received one of the ultimate compliments anyone can get: he was known as "a man after God's own heart." Wow! Wouldn't it be awesome if you were known as a person after God's own heart?

David went boldly into battle against his enemies—after consulting with God. He had an attitude that I love: it was as if he were saying, "God is all I need—let the giants fall where they may! God rocks!"

Prior to fighting Goliath, he demanded, "Who is this un-circumcised Philistine that he should defy the armies of the living God?" (1 Samuel 17:26). What an awesome line!

When the competition, your own sin, or the devil (who comes to steal, kill, and destroy) tries to assault your life, put a little "God rocks!" in your strategy. Cry out in confidence, as David did, "Who are you to defy a son [or daughter] of the living God?"

Prior to going out to fight Goliath (1 Samuel 17:34–39) we read about a young David who had experience with trusting God and seeing Him come through—he trusted Him and had *faith*. Because of this faith, David went to fight Goliath with the weapons he had—skills God had already given him to use against a lion and a bear to protect his father's sheep.

King Saul tried to protect David with his own tunic, a coat of armor, and a bronze helmet. David didn't trust Saul's armor and sword; he trusted the weapons he had, and most particularly he trusted the Lord. So should you—you are a salesperson, and you have incredible gifts—but you also have an incredible God. David knew his own skills, and he knew his weapons, but most important, he knew his God. When you face the giants in your life, face them with the abilities God gave you and has already used, but at the same time, don't forget your God. Remember, "God rocks!" can be pretty powerful when you are slaying your greatest fears.

David said to the Philistine, "You come against me with sword and spear and javelin, but I come against you in the name of the LORD Almighty, the God of the armies of Israel, whom you have defied. This day the LORD will hand you over to me, and I'll strike you down and cut off your head. Today I will give the carcasses of the Philistine army to the birds of the air and the beasts of the earth, and the whole world will know that there is a God in Israel. All those gathered here will know that it is not by sword or spear that the LORD saves; for the battle is the LORD's, and he will give all of you into our hands." (1 Samuel 17:45–47)

These were David's words to Goliath as he pitted his weapons against the giant's. What do you hear in his words as you read them? I hear faith and confidence—and that combination saved the day!

But let me share an eternal truth with you. Remember from Day Eight's Battle Plan you learned that God keeps His promises? Remember He told the enemy that one day He would provide a "headcrusher"? Do you know that David could not have failed if he'd wanted to fail? Why? Because it was in God's plan for David to succeed so that Jesus Christ would be born from David's line! What great purpose might God have in store for you? David's confidence was God-breathed.

Notice David's formula for battlefield success: he prepared for battle, went with his own strengths, acknowledged that the battle was the Lord's, and then delivered on his promise. Boy, did he ever close that deal! You have that same strength available to you from God Almighty today. You truly can do all things through Christ who strengthens you (Philippians 4:13).

Now as the final part of preparation, make sure that you put on the full armor of God, which we find in Ephesians 6:13–18, *every day*. Here's a prayer to help you "dress" for eternal success:

Dear God, today I put on Your full armor, so when evil comes, I'll be able to stand my ground. After I have done this, dear God, I am fully confident that with Your help, I will be able to stand against the enemy . . .

- *with the belt of truth buckled around my waist,*
- *encased in the breastplate of righteousness,*
- *walking in the shoes of the gospel of peace,*
- *bearing Your shield that defeats every missile,*
- *wearing the salvation You gave me as a helmet,*
- *with Your Word ready on my tongue,*
- *praying in the Spirit on all occasions with all kinds of prayers and requests,*
- *on the alert, always ready to pray for others!*

I leave you with two parting Scripture passages. Take a look at Philippians 4:4–9 and pay special attention to the order of the things that Paul laid out:

Rejoice in the Lord always. I will say it again: Rejoice! Let your gentleness be evident to all. The Lord is near. Do not be anxious about anything, but in everything, by prayer and petition, with thanksgiving, present your requests to God. And the peace of God, which transcends all understanding, will guard your hearts and your minds in Christ Jesus.

Finally, brothers, whatever is true, whatever is noble,

whatever is right, whatever is pure, whatever is lovely, whatever is admirable—if anything is excellent or praise-worthy—think about such things. Whatever you have learned or received or heard from me, or seen in me—put it into practice. And the God of peace will be with you.

God's gift to you, as a Christian in sales, is that He will reveal a divine assignment to you even while you are crawling through the jungle and you wonder whether or not the enemy is just a heartbeat away.

Be obedient to the Lord God. Look for Him in every situation, and using these verses, learn to be content in the awesome plan God has for your life:

I am not saying this because I am in need, for I have learned to be content whatever the circumstances. I know what it is to be in need, and I know what it is to have plenty. I have learned the secret of being content in any and every situation, whether well fed or hungry, whether living in plenty or in want. *I can do everything through him who gives me strength.* (Philippians 4:11–13, *emphasis added*)

Thank you for joining me in the study of these daily battle plans. Now, I expect you to run the race and fight the good fight! And remember, arm yourself with the knowledge and conviction that God has an eternal plan for you that exceeds any sales plan you could ever be assigned.

Know the God of the universe as your Savior, and serve Him as you share His story with others!

Day Twenty-two Prayer

Dear God,

I believe that Jesus Christ stands right beside me today and every day and that from Him I receive all the strength I need. When I talk to my customers, help me to have confidence that He is with me then, just as surely as in my quiet time. Give me strength to push through when my own strength has long ended and only Yours remains. When I need rest, let me rest in the arms of Jesus, knowing that I will receive the healing I need.

When I need guidance, help me to seek out Your almighty, all-knowing presence, and boldly, yet humbly, approach Your throne as Your child. Grant me the peace I always receive from Your guidance.

Thank You, God, for the protection You give me—the armor in which You wrap me. For You are my high tower and my sure defense; I will run to You even as the vines of the jungle reach out and try to trip me up . . . trusting in You as my True Vine.

Oh, God, I love You so much. You are always faith-ful. I praise Your holy name. I ask You to come against any

*adversity aimed at me so that no weapon formed against me
will prosper. Today, I run into the battle singing Your praises.
I can do all things as You strengthen me!*

*Help me remember that I work for You, God, and not
men.*

*And finally, help me to remember throughout my life
what You have taught me within this study.*

In Jesus' name. Amen!

Day Twenty-two: My Thoughts

It is harder for us to accomplish some
tasks than others. List some of your
hardest ones here, and trust that through
Jesus Christ's love you can now expect
lasting victory. Move from victim to
victor, tackle the tough issues, and
never again be subject to:

1. _____

   (Christ strengthens me to beat this!)

2. _____

   (Jesus has already won this battle for me!)

3. _____

   (The battle is God's—not mine!)

4. _____

(No weapon formed against me shall prosper!)

5. _____

(This day the Lord will hand you over to me,
and I'll strike you down and cut off your head!)

Jesus, thank You for Your sacrifice of
leaving heaven for me. Today I will make
my sales with You in my heart. Help me to:

_____
_____
_____
_____
_____
_____

Day Twenty-two Prayer Requests

_____
_____
_____
_____
_____
_____

"For I know the plans I have for you,"
*declares the L*ORD*, "plans to prosper you*
and not to harm you, plans to give you
hope and a future."

Jeremiah 29:11

PART TWO

———

Jungle Warfare Field Support

BASIC FIELD MANUAL

■ *b.* Prior to the initiation of operations in jungle areas, a careful analysis of the terrain must be made to determine the practicability of transporting and employing the various organic infantry weapons within each area of operations. Based upon this analysis and the mission, task forces are organized so as to assure maximum tactical mobility and combat effectiveness.

Field Support Introduction

The twenty-two battle plans in this Field Sales Manual are there for your ongoing study, reflection, and growth. Refer back to them and add to your answers as you notice God's hand continuing to guide you. Make special notes and thank Him for the prayer requests He answers. You might also prayerfully consider whether you could serve others by leading them through the twenty-two-day study as well.

This section, Part Two is akin to your own personal, field-issued first aid kit. It provides questions that are often prompted by an acute need by those of us who work in sales. The primary answers provided are the best medicine possible: Scripture.

Prior to utilizing this section, note that the excerpt from Granddad's WWII field manual suggests that you understand the terrain thoroughly *before* engaging in any battle. You want to be ready for any action, be it a skirmish or full-scale war, so a careful analysis of your sales goals, your spiritual goals, and the enemies you may face is essential for your eventual success.

This section serves as your quick-reference guide and will be most effective if you read through it *before* you really need it . . . we all know it's hard to put up a tent in the rain for the first time! The topics within this section are focused on difficult situations and encourage you to build your faith on prayer, God's Word, the Holy Spirit's prompting, a dedication to discipline, and a thankfulness for God's grace.

May God bless you with His love and provision as you seek

His perfect guidance to help you navigate through the dense thicket of the sales jungle.

How does God feel about abundance?

God has the only perfect perspective on wealth and rewards. It's important to see these things, which can be so easily abused, from His vantage point. Read Matthew 19:16–26—and remember that Jesus says at the end of the story, "With man this is impossible, but with God all things are possible" (v. 26).

> "Do not think me mad. It is not to make money that I believe a Christian should live. The noblest thing a man can do is, just humbly to receive, and then go amongst others and give."
>
> David Livingstone

Now read the Scriptures that follow, and consider God's thoughts on abundance.

1 Timothy 6:10

For the love of money is a root of all kinds of evil. Some people, eager for money, have wandered from the faith and pierced themselves with many griefs.

Proverbs 10:4 NLT

Lazy people are soon poor; hard workers get rich.

Riches can give us some godlike attributes, so keep God, not wealth, on the throne of your life.

What is a Christian to do with alcohol or even drugs?

Paul's writings tell us that all things are permitted us under grace, but not all things are profitable. We all know people who have abused something—alcohol, drugs, even food. They run to it instead of God. Anything that you run to instead of Him is an idol in your life. What controls you, and what would you fight to protect?

> *"Wise leaders should have known that the human heart cannot exist in a vacuum. If Christians are forbidden to enjoy the wine of the Spirit they will turn to the wine of the flesh . . . Christ died for our hearts and the Holy Spirit wants to come and satisfy them."*
>
> A. W. Tozer

Proverbs 23:20-21

Do not join those who drink too much wine or gorge themselves on meat, for drunkards and gluttons become poor, and drowsiness clothes them in rags.

1 Timothy 3:3 NLT

He [*an elder*] must not be a heavy drinker or be violent. He must be gentle, not quarrelsome, and not love money.

Ephesians 5:18 NLT

Don't be drunk with wine, because that will ruin your life. Instead, be filled with the Holy Spirit.

Sin is an illegitimate solution to a legitimate need. Make God your solution.

Is it okay for a Christian to be angry?

Everyone gets angry. It is part of the human condition. What we *do* with that anger, however, is important—in fact, it's vital to our relationships with God.

Jesus got angry. He was righteously indignant and drove people out of the temple with a *whip*. His anger was righteous because the sales merchants and priests had turned God's house into a commercial operation instead of a house of worship. He cautioned us against being angry and failing to forgive one another. In Matthew 5, Jesus said:

> You have heard that our ancestors were told, "You must not murder. If you commit murder, you are subject to judgment." But I say, if you are even angry with someone, you are subject to judgment! If you call someone an idiot, you are in danger of being brought before the court. And if you curse someone, you are in danger of the fires of hell.
>
> So if you are presenting a sacrifice at the altar in the Temple and you suddenly remember that someone has something against you, leave your sacrifice there at the altar. Go and be reconciled to that person. Then come and offer your sacrifice to God.
>
> When you are on the way to court with your adversary, settle your differences quickly. Otherwise, your accuser may hand you over to the judge, who will hand you over to an officer, and you will be thrown into prison. And if that happens, you surely won't be free again until you have paid the last penny. (Matthew 5:21–26 NLT)

"*Anyone can become angry—that is easy. But to be angry with the right person, to the right degree, at the right time, for the right purpose, and in the right way—this is not easy.*"

Aristotle

Ephesians 4:26, 31 ESV

Be angry and do not sin; do not let the sun go down on your anger . . . Let all bitterness and wrath and anger and clamor and slander be put away from you, along with all malice.

1 Corinthians 13:5

[*Love*] is not rude, it is not self-seeking, it is not easily angered, it keeps no record of wrongs.

Matthew 5:21-22

You have heard that it was said to the people long ago, "Do not murder, and anyone who murders will be subject to judgment." But I tell you that anyone who is angry with his brother will be subject to judgment.

Forgiveness is setting the prisoner free . . . and realizing that prisoner was you.

Does God care about
my sales numbers?

We often find it easier to believe God for bigger needs and
neglect to petition Him for the small ones. God cares about
everything that weighs on your heart. However, Jesus cautions
us about being preoccupied with the concerns of this life. Read
the parable of the sower in Matthew 13:1–23, paying particular attention to verses 21–23:

> Later that same day Jesus left the house and sat beside the
> lake. A large crowd soon gathered around him, so he got
> into a boat. Then he sat there and taught as the people
> stood on the shore. He told many stories in the form of
> parables, such as this one:
>
> "Listen! A farmer went out to plant some seeds. As he
> scattered them across his field, some seeds fell on a foot-
> path, and the birds came and ate them. Other seeds fell
> on shallow soil with underlying rock. The seeds sprouted
> quickly because the soil was shallow. But the plants soon
> wilted under the hot sun, and since they didn't have deep
> roots, they died. Other seeds fell among thorns that grew
> up and choked out the tender plants. Still other seeds
> fell on fertile soil, and they produced a crop that was
> thirty, sixty, and even a hundred times as much as had

been planted! Anyone with ears to hear should listen and understand."

His disciples came and asked him, "Why do you use parables when you talk to the people?"

He replied, "You are permitted to understand the secrets of the Kingdom of Heaven, but others are not. To those who listen to my teaching, more understanding will be given, and they will have an abundance of knowledge. But for those who are not listening, even what little understanding they have will be taken away from them. That is why I use these parables,

For they look, but they don't really see.
They hear, but they don't really listen or understand.

This fulfills the prophecy of Isaiah that says,

'When you hear what I say,
    you will not understand.
When you see what I do,
    you will not comprehend.
For the hearts of these people are hardened,
    and their ears cannot hear,
and they have closed their eyes—
    so their eyes cannot see,

and their ears cannot hear,
    and their hearts cannot understand,
and they cannot turn to me
    and let me heal them.'

"But blessed are your eyes, because they see; and your ears, because they hear. I tell you the truth, many prophets and righteous people longed to see what you see, but they didn't see it. And they longed to hear what you hear, but they didn't hear it.

"Now listen to the explanation of the parable about the farmer planting seeds: The seed that fell on the footpath represents those who hear the message about the Kingdom and don't understand it. Then the evil one comes and snatches away the seed that was planted in their hearts. The seed on the rocky soil represents those who hear the message and immediately receive it with joy. But since they don't have deep roots, they don't last long. They fall away as soon as they have problems or are persecuted for believing God's word. The seed that fell among the thorns represents those who hear God's word, but all too quickly the message is crowded out by the worries of this life and the lure of wealth, so no fruit is produced. The seed that fell on good soil represents those who truly hear and understand God's word and produce a harvest of thirty, sixty, or even a hundred times as much as had been planted!" (NLT)

> "*The branch of the vine does not worry, and toil, and rush here to seek for sunshine, and there to find rain. No; it rests in union and communion with the vine; and at the right time, and in the right way, is the right fruit found on it. Let us so abide in the Lord Jesus.*"
>
> Hudson Taylor

Mark 11:24 MSG

I urge you to pray for absolutely everything, ranging from small to large. Include everything as you embrace this God-life, and you'll get God's everything.

1 Peter 5:7 NLT

Give all your worries and cares to God, for he cares about you.

Luke 12:29-31 NLT

And don't be concerned about what to eat and what to drink. Don't worry about such things. These things dominate the thoughts of unbelievers all over the world, but your Father already knows your needs. Seek the Kingdom of God above all else, and he will give you everything you need.

God cares about what matters to you; your job is caring about what matters to God.

What is a Christian to do with the competition?

Some have implied that Christians and even Christ Himself are pushovers. Christ's meekness is all-powerful because He relies completely on God for His strength. We of the sales world know that the meek will inherit the earth, but pushovers do not inherit *anything*. If you want to succeed, you must compete—but our lesson comes from Jesus Himself, who said He could only do what the Father wanted Him to do. We are called to compete under God's leadership. So what does God think about sticking it to the competition?

1 Peter 3:15-17

> Always be prepared to give an answer to everyone who asks you to give the reason for the hope that you have. But do this with gentleness and respect, keeping a clear conscience, so that those who speak maliciously against your good behavior in Christ may be ashamed of their slander. It is better, if it is God's will, to suffer for doing good than for doing evil.

> "*I believe in courtesy, in kindness, in generosity, in good cheer, in friendship and in honest competition. I believe there is something doing somewhere, for every man ready to do it. I believe I'm ready, RIGHT NOW.*"
>
> Elbert Hubbard

Psalm 3:3-8 NLT

But you, O LORD, are a shield around me; you are my glory, the one who holds my head high. I cried out to the LORD, and he answered me from his holy mountain . . .

I lay down and slept, yet I woke up in safety, for the LORD was watching over me.

I am not afraid of ten thousand enemies who surround me on every side. Arise, O LORD! Rescue me, my God! Slap all my enemies in the face! Shatter the teeth of the wicked! Victory comes from you, O LORD. May you bless your people.

Always remember: God is with you. And if He is with you, who can be against you (Romans 8:31)?

Is it okay to ask God for courage and sales?

Some of our prayers can be selfish, and the Word cautions us about asking with wrong motives (see James 4:2–3). However, the Lord knows your needs—even before you ask Him! So search your heart when you ask God for sales, and take courage: He is with you. Seek God first. Pour out your heart to Him. He is more concerned about your growth than He is about your success. Grow first—then, succeed in Him.

> *"Ask, and it shall be given you; seek, and ye shall find; knock, and it shall be opened unto you."*
>
>   Jesus Christ

Ephesians 3:12 NLT

Because of Christ and our faith in him, we can now come boldly and confidently into God's presence.

Hebrews 13:6

The Lord is my helper; I will not be afraid. What can man do to me?

1 John 5:15

> And if we know that he hears us—whatever we ask—we know that we have what we asked of him.

We know that we can make our requests to Him and that He will answer us!

What if my customers don't like me?

No matter how charming, how engaging, and how friendly you are, somewhere out there are people who may not like you. Most of us in sales are unused to being disliked, and it can disturb the balance of our universe. However, we have the most important Friend there is.

> *"All my friends are but one, but He is all sufficient."*
>
> **William Carey**

Proverbs 18:24 NKJV

> A man who has friends must himself be friendly, but there is a friend who sticks closer than a brother.

John 15:15

> I no longer call you servants, because a servant does not
> know his master's business. Instead, I have called you
> friends, for everything that I learned from my Father I
> have made known to you.

Romans 5:11 NLT

> So now we can rejoice in our wonderful new relationship
> with God because our Lord Jesus Christ has made us friends
> of God.

Do not worry about pleasing men—the God of the universe is your Friend.

What do I do
when I get depressed or burned-out?

I have sometimes called this the Monday Morning Blues, but
for some people depression and burnout have much deeper
roots. When we are depressed, we must seek God for our
answer—He has provided for our healing in every way, and
in Him is *abundant* life (see John 10:10). Read through the
Psalms. David and the other psalmists went through deep
despair, fear, and doubt—they called upon God in the midst of
their angst, and I have found their honest language refreshing.

> *"If I feel depressed I will sing. If I feel sad I will laugh. If I feel ill I will double my labor. If I feel fear I will plunge ahead. If I feel inferior I will wear new garments. If I feel uncertain I will raise my voice. If I feel poverty I will think of wealth to come. If I feel incompetent I will think of past success. If I feel insignificant I will remember my goals. Today I will be the master of my emotions."*
>
> Og Mandino

Psalm 30:5 NIV

Weeping may remain for a night, but rejoicing comes in the morning.

Psalm 40:2 NKJV

He also brought me up out of a horrible pit, out of the miry clay, and set my feet upon a rock, and established my steps.

Psalm 112:4

Even in darkness light dawns for the upright, for the gracious and compassionate and righteous man.

Isaiah 58:10

> If you spend yourselves in behalf of the hungry and
> satisfy the needs of the oppressed, then your light will
> rise in the darkness, and your night will become like the
> noonday.

God won't leave you in your pit. The darkest night comes
before the dawn. Seek His face. Cry out to Him. He will
answer you.

I feel alone. What should I do?

We often worry about our loved ones while we are away,
and sometimes the burden of being far from them can seem
unbearable. Yet we must remember that God is not only *with
us*; He is *with them*. He is your constant companion and
connection to your family. Picture the face of your favorite
people, and say one deep prayer for each one. Through prayer
God will connect you to their hearts, and your own spirits
will rise.

> "Shakespeare, Leonardo Da Vinci, Benjamin Franklin, and Lincoln never saw a movie, heard a radio, or looked at a TV. They had loneliness and knew what to do with it. They were not afraid of being lonely because they knew that was when the creative mood in them would mark."
>
> Carl Sa

Deuteronomy 31:8

The LORD himself goes before you and will be with you; he will never leave you nor forsake you. Do not be afraid; do not be discouraged.

Joshua 1:5

I will never leave you nor forsake you.

Isaiah 49:15-16

Can a mother forget the baby at her breast and have no compassion on the child she has borne? Though she may forget, I will not forget you! See, I have engraved you on the palms of my hands.

> *"There is none more lonely*
> *than the man who loves only himself."*
>
> Abraham Esra

I compromised my integrity.
What do I do now?

It is interesting to note that God forgives more easily than most people. You can repent to Him and He will forgive you and make it as though you never sinned. That does not mean, however, that our sins have no repercussions. It might be harder to regain someone's trust than to ask God to forgive, but you can earn it back with consistency and honesty.

> *"Have the courage to say no. Have the courage to face*
> *the truth. Do the right thing because it is right. These*
> *are the magic keys to living your life with integrity."*
>
> W. Clement Stone

2 Samuel 22:26 NLT

To the faithful you show yourself faithful; to those with integrity you show integrity.

Psalm **26:11** NKJV

> But as for me, I will walk in my integrity; redeem me and be merciful to me.

Proverbs **2:20** MSG

> So—join the company of good men and women, keep your feet on the tried-and-true paths. It's the men who walk straight who will settle this land, the women with integrity who will last here. The corrupt will lose their lives; the dishonest will be gone for good.

Friendship will earn confidence, but you cannot have true friendship without integrity.

Sometimes my job seems so hard. What do I do?

Sales can be grueling—intense pressure, difficult hours, and frequent temptations to take the easy way out by compromising on our principles hound our days and nights. However, we have a resource unique to Christians: Jesus in our lives gives us His strength. If times are particularly hard, realize that we are not promised a life full of constant sunshine. In your suffering find one small thing to be thankful for and cling to it, nurture it, protect it until God sends you more resources—and He will send you more help. He will never leave you or forsake you.

> *"Courage is grace under pressure."*
>
> Ernest Hemingway

Jonah 2:2

In my distress I called to the LORD, and he answered me. From the depths of the grave I called for help, and you listened to my cry.

Isaiah 46:4

Even to your old age and gray hairs I am he, I am he who will sustain you. I have made you and I will carry you; I will sustain you and I will rescue you.

Romans 5:3-5

Not only so, but we also rejoice in our sufferings, because we know that suffering produces perseverance; perseverance, character; and character, hope. And hope does not disappoint us, because God has poured out his love into our hearts by the Holy Spirit, whom he has given us.

When you reach the edge of your limits, you will see how God provides.

What do I do when stepping out into something new?

Though we often want detailed plans from God before we take a new step, we do not always receive specific instructions no matter how hard we seek them. During these times, we must trust that God is with us and that He is at work, even when we do not see or hear Him.

"Man cannot discover new oceans unless he has the courage to lose sight of the shore."

Andre Gide

Proverbs 16:3, 9

Commit to the LORD whatever you do, and your plans will succeed . . . In his heart a man plans his course, but the LORD determines his steps.

Proverbs 3:5-6

Trust in the LORD with all your heart and lean not on your own understanding; in all your ways acknowledge him, and he will make your paths straight.

James 4:13-15 NKJV

> Come now, you who say, "Today or tomorrow we will go to such and such a city, spend a year there, buy and sell, and make a profit"; whereas you do not know what will happen tomorrow. For what is your life? It is even a vapor that appears for a little time and then vanishes away. Instead you ought to say, "If the Lord wills, we shall live and do this or that."

> *"The undertaking of a new action brings new strength."*
>
> Evenus

I just lost my job! What happens now?

Most of us are not in sales for our health; we are providing for our families. It is very difficult to lose the source of our provision—or *is* it our source? It is easy to see our jobs as our providers, but that is not entirely true. *God* is our supplier. Your Father in heaven sees your plight, and He will provide for all your needs. Regroup by recommitting to recognizing His voice. Seek His guidance, and thank Him for all that He provides.

> "*Every minute starts an hour and every minute is a new opportunity. Each time the clock ticks you have a chance to start over, to say, do, think, or feel something in such a way that you and the world are better for it.*"
>
> Unknown

Psalm 107: 13-16, 19-21

Then they cried to the LORD in their trouble, and he saved them from their distress. He brought them out of darkness and the deepest gloom and broke away their chains. Let them give thanks to the LORD for his unfailing love and his wonderful deeds for men, for he breaks down gates of bronze and cuts through bars of iron . . . Then they cried to the LORD in their trouble, and he saved them from their distress. He sent forth his word and healed them; he rescued them from the grave. Let them give thanks to the LORD for his unfailing love and his wonderful deeds for men.

Luke 12: 29-30

Do not set your heart on what you will eat or drink; do not worry about it. For the pagan world runs after all such things, and your Father knows that you need them.

> "*Vitality shows not only in the ability to persist but in the ability to start over.*"
>
> Unknown

What do I do when I don't feel thankful or satisfied?

The wisest man alive encountered this same problem—he had everything, yet he found that he was not content. Solomon penned that nothing could satisfy him and that everything was meaningless. Yet he made an addendum—all is meaningless without *God*. This is true of your life, too, and your only hope is deciding to be thankful to Him and to praise Him for what He's done.

> "*If a fellow isn't thankful for what he's got, he isn't likely to be thankful for what he's going to get.*"
>
> Frank A. Clark
>
> "*The worst moment for the atheist is when he is really thankful and has nobody to thank.*"
>
> Dante Rossetti

Philippians 4:11-12 MSG

I've learned by now to be quite content whatever my circumstances. I'm just as happy with little as with much, with much as with little. I've found the recipe for being happy whether full or hungry, hands full or hands empty. Whatever I have, wherever I am, I can make it through anything in the One who makes me who I am.

1 Timothy 6:8

But if we have food and clothing, we will be content with that.

1 Peter 5:6 MSG

So be content with who you are, and don't put on airs. God's strong hand is on you; he'll promote you at the right time. Live carefree before God; he is most careful with you.

"God has two dwellings; one in heaven, and the other in a meek and thankful heart."

Izaak Walton

God, will You please help me?

We all reach times of desperation—sometimes it is so bad, all we can do is cry, "God, help!" When you are in one of these situations, it's important to remember to whom you are praying: the all-powerful, all-knowing, all-compassionate God who saved you, called you His own, and redeemed you. He hears you and is ready to commune with you. Go to Him now and receive His blessing.

> *"Here I stand; I can do no other. God help me. Amen!"*
>
> Martin Luther

Psalm 77:1, 5, 6, 11–14

I cried out to God for help; I cried out to God to hear me . . . I thought about the former days; the years of long ago; I remembered my songs in the night. . . . I will remember the deeds of the LORD; yes, I will remember your miracles of long ago. I will meditate on all your works and consider all your mighty deeds. Your ways, O God, are holy. What god is so great as our God? You are the God who performs miracles; you display your power among the peoples.

1 John 5:14-15

> This is the confidence we have in approaching God: that
> if we ask anything according to his will, he hears us. And
> if we know that he hears us—whatever we ask—we know
> that we have what we asked of him.

It's okay to run out of words—you only need one, anyway:
Jesus.

What do I do when faced with sexual temptation?

First, read Proverbs 6:20–35 and Proverbs 7:1–27 and let me
emphasize that these verses are about all people, both men and
women, who seek to pull you into immorality. Lust and infi-
delity are not gender specific. The most beautiful thing you
ever see will probably be the devil him- or herself.

> *My son, obey your father's commands,*
>   *and don't neglect your mother's instruction.*
> *Keep their words always in your heart.*
>   *Tie them around your neck.*

When you walk, their counsel will lead you.
  When you sleep, they will protect you.
  When you wake up, they will advise you.
For their command is a lamp
  and their instruction a light;
their corrective discipline
  is the way to life.
It will keep you from the immoral woman,
  from the smooth tongue of a promiscuous woman.
Don't lust for her beauty.
  Don't let her coy glances seduce you.
For a prostitute will bring you to poverty,
  but sleeping with another man's wife will cost you
      your life.
Can a man scoop a flame into his lap
  and not have his clothes catch on fire?
Can he walk on hot coals
  and not blister his feet?
So it is with the man who sleeps with another man's wife.
  He who embraces her will not go unpunished.
Excuses might be found for a thief
  who steals because he is starving.
But if he is caught, he must pay back seven times
  what he stole,
  even if he has to sell everything in his house.

But the man who commits adultery is an utter fool,
for he destroys himself.
He will be wounded and disgraced.
His shame will never be erased.
For the woman's jealous husband will be furious,
and he will show no mercy when he takes revenge.
He will accept no compensation,
nor be satisfied with a payoff of any size.

Proverbs 6:20-35 NLT

Now, consider these additional words from Proverbs:

Follow my advice, my son;
always treasure my commands.
Obey my commands and live!
Guard my instructions as you guard your own eyes.
Tie them on your fingers as a reminder.
Write them deep within your heart.
Love wisdom like a sister;
make insight a beloved member of your family.
Let them protect you from an affair with an immoral
woman,
from listening to the flattery of a promiscuous woman.

While I was at the window of my house,
  looking through the curtain,
I saw some naive young men,
and one in particular who lacked common sense.
He was crossing the street near the house of an
    immoral woman,
  strolling down the path by her house.
It was at twilight, in the evening,
  as deep darkness fell.
The woman approached him,
  seductively dressed and sly of heart.
She was the brash, rebellious type,
  never content to stay at home.
She is often in the streets and markets,
  soliciting at every corner.
She threw her arms around him and kissed him,
  and with a brazen look she said,
"I've just made my peace offerings
  and fulfilled my vows.
You're the one I was looking for!
  I came out to find you, and here you are!
My bed is spread with beautiful blankets,
  with colored sheets of Egyptian linen.
I've perfumed my bed
  with myrrh, aloes, and cinnamon.

Come, let's drink our fill of love until morning.
   Let's enjoy each other's caresses,
for my husband is not home.
   He's away on a long trip.
He has taken a wallet full of money with him
and won't return until later this month."

So she seduced him with her pretty speech
   and enticed him with her flattery.
He followed her at once,
   like an ox going to the slaughter.
He was like a stag caught in a trap,
   awaiting the arrow that would pierce its heart.
He was like a bird flying into a snare,
   little knowing it would cost him his life.
So listen to me, my sons,
   and pay attention to my words.
Don't let your hearts stray away toward her.
   Don't wander down her wayward path.
For she has been the ruin of many;
   many men have been her victims.
Her house is the road to the grave.
   Her bedroom is the den of death.

                        Proverbs 7:1-27 NLT

Sexual temptation is one of the most prevalent and successful of the devil's attacks on people (especially men). He preys on this basic instinct, using it against us. If we rely on our own strength to face the devil's temptation, we will fall. But we have the Holy Spirit within us, and Jesus Christ is our strength!

> "Trials, temptations, disappointments—all these are helps instead of hindrances, if one uses them rightly. They not only test the fiber of character but strengthen it. Every conquering temptation represents a new fund of moral energy. Every trial endured and weathered in the right spirit makes a soul nobler and stronger than it was before."
>
> James Buckham

Titus 3:3-7

At one time we too were foolish, disobedient, deceived and enslaved by all kinds of passions and pleasures. We lived in malice and envy, being hated and hating one another. But when the kindness and love of God our Savior appeared, he saved us, not because of righteous things we had done, but because of his mercy. He saved us through the washing of rebirth and renewal by the Holy Spirit, whom he poured out on us generously through Jesus Christ our Savior, so that, having been justified by his grace, we might become heirs having the hope of eternal life.

2 Timothy 2:22 NLT

Run from anything that stimulates youthful lusts. Instead, pursue righteous living, faithfulness, love, and peace. Enjoy the companionship of those who call on the Lord with pure hearts.

James 4:7 NLT

So humble yourselves before God. Resist the devil, and he will flee from you.

"Good habits result from resisting temptation."

Ancient Proverb

I feel lost. What do I do next?

There are going to be times when you simply feel lost and without direction. The heavens may seem as brass, and you might think your prayers are bouncing back in your face. When in these situations, first check your heart—ask God to search you and forgive you of any hidden sin. Be still before Him and step out when you have peace.

> *"I want to know God's thoughts . . . the rest are details."*
>
> Albert Einstein

Psalm 139:23

Search me, O God, and know my heart; test me and know my anxious thoughts.

Jeremiah 17:9 MSG

The heart is hopelessly dark and deceitful, a puzzle that no one can figure out. But I, God, search the heart and examine the mind. I get to the heart of the human. I get to the root of things. I treat them as they really are, not as they pretend to be.

Proverbs 4:18

The path of the righteous is like the first gleam of dawn, shining ever brighter till the full light of day.

Faith is stepping out when you are lost and do not know where your foot will fall.

What do I do with success?

Success is a peculiar thing because people strive for it so hard but then react to it in many different ways. Some lose sight of their origins; others can only think of the next mountain to climb. When you achieve success, thank God for it. He has been with you the whole way!

> *"Success is not measured by what you accomplish, but by the opposition you have encountered, and the courage with which you have maintained the struggle against overwhelming odds."*
>
> Orison Swett Marden

2 Corinthians 3:5 NLT

It is not that we think we are qualified to do anything on our own. Our qualification comes from God.

James 1:17

Every good and perfect gift is from above, coming down from the Father of the heavenly lights, who does not change like shifting shadows.

Psalm 103:2-5

> Praise the LORD, O my soul, and forget not all his benefits—who forgives all your sins and heals all your diseases, who redeems your life from the pit and crowns you with love and compassion, who satisfies your desires with good things so that your youth is renewed like the eagle's.

No rules for success will work if you don't give thanks to God for blessing you.

How can I learn to work hard or stay motivated?

Salespeople without a good work ethic often find themselves forcibly looking for other lines of work. We must be self-motivated, innovative, and constantly seeking to improve. God put Adam to work in the Garden—it was a job with a purpose ordained by his Creator. And, like all God created, it was good.

> *"We are at our very best, and we are happiest, when we are fully engaged in work we enjoy on the journey toward the goal we've established for ourselves. It gives meaning to our time off and comfort to our sleep. It makes everything else in life so wonderful, so worthwhile."*
>
> **Earl Nightingale**

Genesis 2:15

The LORD God took the man and put him in the Garden of Eden to work it and take care of it.

1 Thessalonians 4:11-12

Make it your ambition to lead a quiet life, to mind your own business and to work with your hands, just as we told you, so that your daily life may win the respect of outsiders and so that you will not be dependent on anybody.

Colossians 3:23-24

Whatever you do, work at it with all your heart, as working for the Lord, not for men, since you know that you will receive an inheritance from the Lord as a reward. It is the Lord Christ you are serving.

God equips each of us with talents; yours is sales. So go forth and sell!

What do I do when I'm exhausted?

Miles to go before you sleep—been there? We all have! I think it's part of the fall of man that we work ourselves to exhaustion yet never seem to finish the tasks before us. Yet unlike those without Christ, we have an inexhaustible reservoir of strength, for Jesus lives within us and *is* our strength. When you are exhausted go back to Section One of this manual and recommit to learning to be still and resting in God (see Day Thirteen).

> *"Give me your tired, your poor, your huddled masses yearning to breathe free, the wretched refuse of your teeming shore. Send these, the homeless, tempest-tost to me, I lift my lamp beside the golden door!"*
>
> Emma Lazarus, excerpt from
> "The Statue of Liberty"

Proverbs 17:22 MSG

A cheerful disposition is good for your health; gloom and doom leave you bone-tired.

Isaiah 40:28-31

Do you not know? Have you not heard? The LORD is the everlasting God, the Creator of the ends of the earth. He will not grow tired or weary, and his understanding no one can fathom. He gives strength to the weary and increases the power of the weak. Even youths grow tired and weary, and young men stumble and fall; but those who hope in the LORD will renew their strength. They will soar on wings like eagles; they will run and not grow weary, they will walk and not be faint.

Hebrews 12:12 NLT

So take a new grip with your tired hands and strengthen your weak knees.

"The soul cannot prosper in spiritual things, without much secret converse with its God and Saviour."

Thomas Shaw B. Reade

What do I do when I'm worried?

There are times when worry dogs your heels and you cannot seem to shake it. There is only one choice—presenting your cares to the Lord, for He cares for you (1 Peter 5:7). But then you must leave them there in His presence and not take them with you when you leave your time of prayer—that's the hard part.

> "I do not worry about the things I can change, for I can change them; I do not worry about the things I cannot change, for I cannot change them. Therefore, I do not worry."
>
> Unknown

Matthew 6:27, 32-34 NLT

Can all your worries add a single moment to your life? . . . Your heavenly Father already knows all your needs. Seek the Kingdom of God above all else, and live righteously, and he will give you everything you need. So don't worry about tomorrow, for tomorrow will bring its own worries. Today's trouble is enough for today.

Psalm 23:1-6

The LORD is my shepherd, I shall not want.

He makes me lie down in green pastures, he leads me beside quiet waters, he restores my soul. He guides me in paths of righteousness for his name's sake.

Even though I walk through the valley of the shadow of death, I will fear no evil, for you are with me; your rod and your staff, they comfort me.

You prepare a table before me in the presence of my enemies. You anoint my head with oil; my cup overflows.

Surely goodness and love will follow me all the days of my life, and I will dwell in the house of the LORD forever.

"It is not work that kills, but worry."

African Proverb

--- About the Author ---

Christopher A. Cunningham is a sales professional for one of the nation's leading medical device companies. He has worked at the vice presidential level in sports and entertainment marketing. He is a certified lay minister and speaks to sales and marketing teams (as well as Christian groups) at meetings and retreats about "Believing Impossible Beliefs." He's a happy husband and dad of four great kids. His dog George Bailey is a very special part of his wonderful life. Most of all, he is thankful for the grace and love of his Savior, Jesus Christ, who leads him beside still waters—even in the jungle.

To contact Christopher, write to him at
Chris.halomarketing@gmail.com.

If you would like for him to inspire your group or team, use the e-mail address above.

For information on leading a Jungle Warfare small group session write to Christopher c/o Thomas Nelson Publishers in Nashville, Tennessee.

--- Acknowledgments ---

I'd like to acknowledge God's amazing grace in my life—
"how sweet the sound that saved a wretch like me. I once
was lost but now I'm found—was blind but now I see." Those
words have resonated deeply within my soul since I went to
church camp as a young boy and returned home singing them
with great conviction. My parents Mac and Joan (and my
grandparents) nurtured the Holy Spirit within me, and it con-
tinues to produce fruit in my life like the privilege of writing
this book. His amazing grace provides a sacred, spiritual quick-
ening in my relationship with my wife, Heather. His mercy
gives me a song in my heart to pray daily for my own dear
children . . . and to be able to give thanks for doing my work
well. Many heartfelt thanks go to Joel Miller, my publisher, and
Kristen Parrish, my editor, for their belief in me and this proj-
ect. Their dedication and honest commitment made this book
smarter, fresher, and wiser. I wouldn't want to go through the
jungle without them or without God's love; His son, Jesus; or
the holy fire He has put inside my soul.